Connie Dever's book *He Will H*
penetrating and deeply moving. I love
passages and quotations through her story.

ELIZABETH CATHERWOOD
Eldest daughter of Dr Martyn Lloyd-Jones

After suffering, we often forget how the dark times actually felt. We remember that they happened, that we wondered whether we'd ever laugh again. But how they felt is hard to recall. Yet loving others who suffer requires our empathy. The beauty of Connie's book is that it's her journal – her raw emotions, fears, and hopes – in the midst of her suffering. And, therefore, it's a companion for anyone who is suffering because it remembers the dark times – and the hope we can have in them.

BETHANY L. JENKINS
Director of Every Square Inch
The Gospel Coalition and Director of Vocational & Career
Development, The King's College, New York City, New York

The blogposts of Connie Dever as she pursues her pilgrimage through cancer country on her way to the promised land are the stuff of a spiritual classic: highly reserved yet searingly candid. They are reserved with respect to family, friends, and daily events, but this reserve tends to sharpen the focus on the clarity of Connie's fight against the demons of fear and unbelief. Here is a Christian who wrestles with God and shares her struggles with her readers, a Christian who seeks out the joy of the Lord in the midst of radiation-induced nausea, a Christian who cherishes and knows how to read her Bible, a Christian who is never tempted to portray herself as a fine exemplar of the 'victorious Christian life' but whose sparkling honesty testifies, through the tears, that 'he will hold me fast.'

D. A. CARSON
Research Professor of New Testament
Trinity Evangelical Divinity School in Deerfield, Illinois

I remember reading Connie's Facebook posts as she chronicled her journey through cancer. Some days she would post how the Lord was bearing her up, some days she expressed her fears and asked for prayer, some days it was a photo of a beautiful scenery from her mountain retreat offering praise to God for the beauty of His creation. It was indeed a privilege to share in her times of pain and radiation and insomnia, as well as in her seasons of peace and rest. I was strangely drawn to her story as she expressed the raw and real trials and joys that accompany suffering. Even more, I was drawn towards Christ whose tender care and faithfulness was so evident in these journal entries. I believe your heart will be encouraged to persevere in your own trials, to pray for others who are suffering, to praise our Savior for demonstrations of His love and His glory displayed in the big and small, and in the difficult and smooth paths that He places before us.

KRISTIE ANYABWILE
Pastor's wife, Mother of 3, Washington D.C.

a journey with grace through cancer

HE WILL HOLD ME FAST

CONNIE DEVER

CHRISTIAN
FOCUS

paperback ISBN 978-1-78191-985-9
epub ISBN 978-1-52710-015-2
mobi ISBN 978-1-52710-016-9

10 9 8 7 6 5 4 3 2 1

Published in 2017
by
Christian Focus Publications Ltd,
Geanies House, Fearn, Ross-shire,
IV20 1TW, Great Britain.

www.christianfocus.com

Cover design by
Pete Barnsley (Creative Hoot)

Printed and bound by
Bell & Bain, Glasgow

Contents

For Jeff and Sharon Gruber
God has used you to bless me in countless ways
throughout this journey. More than friends;
more like family. Forever grateful.

Foreword

The Christian life is a fight. Often with and within our own hearts. And when we are in the midst of a long war with unabating adverse circumstances, growing weary, discouraged, even hopeless and despairing is one of the battles we face. In those times, nothing is more important than believing God's word and promises. Jesus said: 'Let not your heart be troubled: you believe in God, believe also in me' (John 14:1) and 'These things I have spoken to you, that in me you might have peace. In the world you will have tribulation: but take courage; I have overcome the world' (John 16:33).

And it is especially powerful to receive encouragement from these Scriptural truths via the example, testimony and exhortation of a fellow believer who has gone through similar circumstances. One who speaks from experience. One who is no 'dry land sailor' (as Spurgeon once quipped about those who were ready to give all kinds of advice and counsel to those undergoing things they had never themselves faced – after all, we'd all prefer advice on sailing from a sailor who has sailed!).

Indeed, it can even be helpful to witness the soul struggles of a strong fellow believer to trust God and take

Him at His Word. To arrive by God's grace through faith at hope, and even peace. To believe the promises of God's Word even when all other lights have gone out. Someone to whom we can admit our desperation because we know that they know what we are going through, because we have watched them go through it. Someone from whom we are willing to receive words of counsel and encouragement because we know they understand.

Connie Dever is such a Christian.

I have known Connie (and her husband Mark) for about thirty years now. I was visiting Cambridge, England to preach and a mutual friend introduced me to Mark. We quickly became fast friends, and Mark and Connie welcomed me into their home, to share meals, sing hymns, and talk and talk (about everything!). I was deeply impressed by them from the beginning. Both brilliant Duke grads. Both with hearts for God and ministry. Both extremely gifted and giving – constantly investing themselves in others. I loved (and still love) just being around them.

I have known Mark and Connie long enough and well enough to have prayed for them in significant trials and hard ongoing circumstances. As is usually the case with all of us, some of those trials were unknown to and unseen by many.

However, when Connie was diagnosed with cancer four years ago, she bravely opened up to let friends and congregants follow that fight of faith with her through her personal posts on what she was facing and how she was handling it. I started reading those posts regularly and not only did they inform my prayers for Connie (and

Mark), but I saw in their raw honesty a source of real help and encouragement for others. I am very thankful that someone encouraged Connie to collect them in book form and allow them to encourage a wider circle.

Reading Connie's spiritual diary-like posts through this relentless journey helped me personally and pastorally. They helped me process some of my own struggles and they helped me understand those I serve, especially in their often-hidden battles of the heart.

If you or a loved one is battling cancer, the application and help found here will be obvious. But even if you are not, there is comfort to be gained and wisdom to be learned from Connie's biblically informed reflections on her trials.

May the Father's love, the Son's grace and the Spirit's communion be your help and stay, and may you come to know, even in your tribulations, the peace that passes understanding.

Ligon Duncan
Chancellor/CEO, Reformed Theological Seminary
John E. Richards Professor of Systematic
and Historical Theology

Introduction

> *'You have thyroid cancer,' the doctor told
> me on December 18, 2013. 'We must
> remove your thyroid and assess how far
> the cancer has spread.'*

'No, God!' I gasped. My thoughts immediately jumped to
the possible implications of this diagnosis. What kind of
intense suffering might I be about to face? How could I cope
with the treatment? What if my cancer was terminal? How
could I leave my loved ones and my half-finished dreams?
How would I deal with my own death? These fear-filled
questions swept over me. 'No, God, I can't do this,' I cried.
This was more than I could handle.

And therein lay the crux of the problem: it was more
than I could handle, and I did not like – or feel safe –
depending upon God. I liked (and felt safest) depending
upon myself.

This is an embarrassingly, spiritually juvenile confession
from someone who has known the Lord for forty-five years
and been a pastor's wife for over half that time. After all,
I know God. I believe God's Word. I've seen His goodness

and kindness in remarkable ways throughout my years. Yet nonetheless, I've harbored a distrust, an unrest, a withholding of myself from Him.

Then Came Cancer ...

With the cancer diagnosis came a Grand Canyon-sized discrepancy between what I needed and my own ability to provide it ... and I knew it. I wanted to escape, but couldn't. I had no choice but to walk straight towards what felt like a thousand-foot, mile-wide, sheer drop-off. Undoubtedly, this was exactly what my loving Heavenly Father had in mind for my good; but true-to-form, I was terrified.

In one sense, I was right to be terrified. Life was about to get very difficult. The surgery and radiation treatment themselves were not too bad, but my body's reaction to them was turbulent. I came to learn first-hand the great influence the thyroid and its four little buddies, the parathyroids, have on our bodies. Among other things, these tiny organs help regulate our heart rate, metabolism, mental health, sleep, and muscles. When my thyroid and half my parathyroids were removed, I began to experience severe muscle spasms in my back, arms, and legs. I had heart palpitations and insomnia. For a while my temperature took dips into the 96's, giving me chills that only a tightly-tied hoody and multiple layers of blankets could stop. Worst of all were the roller coaster highs of anxiety and lows of depression as my body over-reacted then under-reacted to the thyroid medicine. Each day brought its own issues. One symptom would resolve only to be replaced by another.

I felt like I was on a stormy sea, gasping for air when another wave would slap me. I was used to troubleshooting my symptoms and finding solutions, but not this time. Now I had to wait, endure and trust myself to doctors and to the God who answers prayer.

My soul echoed my body's turbulence. Everything felt so desperately out of control, especially during the long nights. Alone, in the dark, I struggled with feelings that God had abandoned me. My pain and sleeplessness stood in stark contrast to the quietness of those sleeping soundly in the rest of the house. Fears seized me and sometimes evil felt palpably close.

At times I couldn't even open my Bible – only hold it. I wept in shame at my inability to fight and believe. I knew God's Word! I believed His promises. Why wouldn't they stick to my mind and heart? Why couldn't I stand up to the lies? Why wouldn't I change? I was at the end of myself. 'God, hold on to me! My body, my faith, my sanity!' I prayed. 'You are going to do to this. I can't. I can't do anything'

And hold onto me, He did.

God particularly brought two Scriptures to mind during this time. The first was, 'I am the vine; you are the branches. Whoever abides in me and I in him, he it is that bears much fruit, for apart from me you can do nothing' (John 5:5). The second became my prayer-theme passage: 'He is able to do far more abundantly than all we could ask or think, according to the power within us' (Eph. 3:20).

'You can do nothing.' Ordinarily, this was the ultimate downer for a self-reliant person like me. Yet now, at the end of myself, it was wonderfully encouraging. It meant that my 'to-do-by-myself list' was absolutely blank, but God's 'to-do-with-Him' list was jam-packed. He wasn't there to just fill in the cracks where my own ability wore thin. Instead, He undergirded everything. He supplied the power. Everything depended upon Him – not me. He knew it and planned it that way. He could bring me through this trial, and every other one I would ever face, for my good and His glory.

And how exactly should I define this 'everything' that God could do?

'Everything' was mind-bogglingly big. I could ask and think all day, and it still would not be expansive enough. I began to make a list, asking and thinking as big as I could. I was as excited as a child writing a Christmas letter to Santa – actually more so. This list was not addressed to some mythical person with mythical powers who gave presents to good children once a year. No! This list was for the living, sovereign, omnipotent God who delights to answer the daily needs of His sinful, needy children. He could do anything. (Cue big, greedy grin.)

As you might expect, my list included asking God to heal my body and sustain my life. But this trial had shown me how fleeting this life is and how the things of this world can't bring fulfillment or security. I would only find lasting joy and peace in God and desiring His will, so most of my requests were of a more spiritual nature.

- I didn't want to waste a speck of this trial. I wanted to live gratefully for His goodness shown to me in it.

- I wanted to joyfully surrender my plans, my resources, myself into God's hands, convinced that His ways are better and wiser than mine.

- I wanted God's Word to be woven into the very beat of my heart. I wanted the lies that fed my fears to fall in the wake of God's truth.

- I wanted to know God so intimately that I could laugh at the days ahead, looking to God's bountiful resources instead of my puny ones to meet them. I wanted to be a bold, risk-taker who saw difficulties as opportunities for God to show His goodness and greatness.

- I wanted other weak and struggling Christians to see God helping me and for them to be encouraged that He would help them, too. I wanted non-Christians to look at what God was doing in me and see His unmistakable power – power enough to even raise the dead!

- I wanted to know that God would always hold onto me. I wanted to rest deeply in His steadfast love for me every day of my life.

It's not that the war is over. My enemies of fear and self-reliance assault me almost daily. I'm not a completely transformed, living-on-a-new-plane-of-existence woman of God. I think that will have to wait until heaven.

But I do have little victories each day – more than before. Even when I don't have victories, I have hope.

- Hope, because I've seen the power of the prayers of the saints as God has answered them in my life.

- Hope, because God's Word is being woven into my heart, growing in power to strike down the enemy's lies.

- Hope, because now I am quicker to surrender my life to God because of a growing certainty that His plans are better, even if they are harder.

- Hope, because I have more confidence that God will give me the power of His Holy Spirit to meet towering difficulties. There is a glimmer of thrill where there used to be only the chill of fear.

- Hope, that God will indeed bring glory to Himself, in the church and through Jesus Christ, even through weak, fearful, needy little me.

- And hope, because He's holding me and holding me fast … and that's far, far better than me holding onto me.

I may have long way to go in this battle with cancer. (Though, praise God, I've received optimistic doctors' reports.) And I certainly have an even longer way to go in this battle with self-reliance. But that's okay. God has done it all before. Maybe He's fighting this battle in you even now. If you are a child of God, take heart. If you are not a child of God, you can become one! Whoever comes to Him, in repentance and faith, He will never cast out (John 6:37). Our confidence is in the God who can do more than we can ask or think. He does not disappoint. Our hope in Him will not put us to shame (Rom. 5:1-5).

Before you go any further...

I love the word 'journey'. It literally means 'a day's portion', but it conjures up the idea of a traveller setting out to somewhere unvisited and faraway. And risk. There's definitely risk involved. The story is as much about what happened on the way there as what happened when you reached your destination. The route took you places you never imagined (or even desired) you would take. The foes were frequently bigger than you thought you could face. The friends you found in unexpected places. And the ugly sores turned into scars that became beauty marks through the whole experience.

This book combines both of these 'du jour/day's portion' and 'traveller's adventure' ideas of journey. They are excerpts from my blog, written over three years as my path took an unexpected turn into cancer. We have kept them very 'du jour' as dated entries through those days as life unfolds. The struggle has been physical, mental, emotion and spiritual. The traveller (me) is a self-acknowledged weakish, trembly sort of creature who loves her comfort zone (a sort-of flunky hobbit), but finds herself a long way out of it . And, while perhaps sputtering and gasping for air, who nonetheless is given not just strength for each battle by the prayers and support of friends, the truth of God's Word, and the grace of God, Himself; but also, the eyes to see that the trials were indeed best gifts from the hand of a wise and loving Father.

I started the blog because I knew my struggle with cancer was not going to be a pretty fight. And, if God could help someone like me, then perhaps others might be encouraged that God does not just help those who soar through difficulties with flying colors, but He stoops, oh so low, to pick up even the most unlikely soul and carry them along in His everlasting arms. To that end, I hope both my weakness and the great and kind strength with which He met me, will grow your confidence in the Lord and see that He, too, can hold you fast.

DIARY
•••••• *2014* ••••••

January 29, 2014

They've come up with a diagnosis for my back. It's called mechanically induced adhesive arachnoiditis. That means that because of my previous back surgeries, nerves in my lower back have begun to join together creating tingling, numbness, weakness and pain. It is pretty scary prognosis if you read up on it.

Life is very overwhelming just now. But I'm learning to slice off little bits at a time and digest those.

As the body crumbles, it reminds me of how clay-like it is. I wish Humpty Dumpty could be put together again… And maybe he will.

But if God will use these crumbles to show Himself to be alive, good, powerful, trustworthy and oh so near, to myself, and to others, then it will be worth it.

January 30 2104

The Doctor has been helpful and given me lots of hope ☺ … He thinks if I'm patient and very good at doing the things he has recommended that I will get better! Even if I don't, apparently they have some new ways to block the nerve messages with something that works like a pacemaker for the spine. Weird huh? Anyway…. Good news!!

February 8, 2014

This has been quite a week! I'm getting ready for my meeting next week with the nuclear med team (regarding radiation therapy); we also received some sad news about some dear friends. BUT oh, how good God has been! Perhaps best of all, He is teaching me so much more about painting the walls of my heart and life with the reality of His truth.

I've been meditating on His truth in a more intense way than ever before, allowing myself (with His help) to see that it really is the reality and the future is oh so bright!

Faith is being certain of that which is unseen. He kindly is giving me more of this kind of faith! I am so grateful!

February 11, 2014

I'm remembering to fight for songs in the night….

So many sleepless nights remind me of the old days when my children were just babies and there were the night feeds, the dirty diapers, the nightmares, teething pains etc. Now it's my own body who is the grumpy customer… Most usually the back or a goofed up calcium level or anxiety…and pain.

I miss the nights of sleeping through and waking up refreshed. They seem to be a thing of the past… At least for now.

Now I need to ask God to help me fight for songs in the night…to use the times awake well.

In the past I learned to arm myself with music, a short Bible verse to chew on and people to pray for. It helped my attitude and it was encouraging to see how God answered many prayers prayed during that time.

Now I'm asking Him again to help me not be the fussy child because I'm awake yet again! But to once more sing in the night…to pray for others, to remember His kindnesses or at least try to have a sweet spirit.

From God's Word:
Psalm 139:17-18

February 11, 2014
Just re-read the binder of information about the radioactive iodine treatment I will be having. Tomorrow at 10:30 is my appointment with the nuclear med docs and I'm armed with my questions.

Ugh!! I am just plain ole scared of the procedure and what the scans will show.

I need to rest in God and His goodness, His control and plan for whatever is ahead! May I go into this seeing it as an opportunity to testify to others about who God is rather than be so consumed with my lack of trust that no one sees anything but me!

February 12, 2014
Long meeting with the nuclear med doctor! At least he was thorough! Thankfully, I wasn't nervous at all.

I was not pleased to hear that it can take up to eight weeks for your blood cell levels to return to normal and that my calcium levels can get all messed up again! Ugh! I keep wishing I could see the end of this cancer portion of my journey but I guess I had better readjust my sights. I think it's one of those vanishing horizons that keep moving further away. Better start making the most of the goodness in each day rather than place my happiness on when this is over!

February 14, 2014
I've been reading what Charles Spurgeon says on God multiplying His consolations to us as our trials increase.

However, this storm is the biggest I have ever been in, and I must say that the 'happiness and consolation' don't FEEL like a palpable closeness to God as I hoped it would.

It feels more like an utter inability to do for myself or rely upon myself for anything. I have to abandon myself to God to carry me. And He does … in remarkable ways. I think that He must tailor our consolations to the work He is doing in our soul.

Mine obviously needs to know that nothing depends on me and all in Him. Happiness is there. And I must say that is deeply consoling to a worry addict like me.

February 16, 2014
Today I see my surgeon and we will talk about my growing difficulty in swallowing and voice issues because of my tightening scar. I'm hoping she has some suggestions.

My respect for a wonky thyroid's effect on one's total body grows daily! They are keeping my thyroid levels high with Meds to keep more cancer from growing and in preparation for the radiation therapy which is good. But I'm jittery and emotional in a way that makes me long for the seemingly easy days of just plain ole being anxious.

I'm praying for wisdom, patience and perseverance… And even a bit of relief. My body and soul are feeling so weary!

From God's Word:
Psalm 66:20
Isaiah 58:8
Isaiah 12:2

February 18, 2014
Thankful! The Doctor is optimistic that my swallowing issues will get better. They are giving me two more weeks for this to clear before they will do anything more about it.

Blood work has been ordered to see if they can straighten out the imbalances that are causing my body and emotions to be so up and down. They are all telling me to be patient; that it can take months. Ugh! Patient and months… Not two words I like to have put together.

So I'm asking God to help me be extra aware of all the ways He shows His love to me each day. That helps me remember He is in control of this storm. He will hold on to me.

From God's Word:
Lamentations 3: 19-26

February 19, 2014
I am praising God for His kindness in giving me a much better night's sleep last night and feeling better today. And

oh how nice it is to see the sun, hear birdies chirping and to feel like winter might actual end one day!

> *From God's Word:*
> His compassions never fail, they are new every morning. LAMENTATIONS 3:23
>
> *Word of Wisdom:*
> God is a faithful Physician, and therefore will turn all to the best. If God does not give you that which you like, He will give you that which you need.
> The physician does not so much study to please the taste of the patient, as to cure his disease.
> God's dealings with His children, though they are sharp, yet they are safe, and in order to cure; that He might do them good. – THOMAS WATSON

February 20, 2014
Turning a corner in my heart? I think...

> There is no fear in love. But Perfect love drives out fear, because fear has to do with punishment. The one who loves is made perfect in love. 1 John 4:18

I'm beginning to think the big reason behind God allowing this physical storm in my life is to put me in a place where I know more of His love for me and, to deepen my love for Him.

I've struggled with understanding how this is God's love: this onslaught of not one but a number of conditions at the same time.

It's led to times of greater fear of Him and even anger towards Him. I'm seeing these future difficulties like punishment, not love.

24

Yet lately, the clouds are parting a bit. While my behavior towards Him certainly would deserve punishment He really is the faithful, patient, merciful lover of my soul.

This morning feels like my heart is thawing and growing in love for Him and in His choosing of this trial.

Instead of pointing my bony finger angrily at Him, I see that I've been the one in the wrong. I so appreciate that His response to me is the same forgiveness, mercy and kindness that it has always been.

Is it possible for perfect love to drive out even my fear? I'm beginning to think that maybe it can! Praise God!

> *Word of Wisdom:*
>
> O Christ, He is the fountain, the deep, sweet well
> of love!
> The streams of earth I've tasted more deep I'll
> drink above:
> There to an ocean fullness His mercy doth expand,
> And glory, glory dwelleth in Immanuel's land.
> *The Sands of Time are Sinking*, ANNE R. COUSIN

February 21, 2014

Prayer Request: Posting this at 2 a.m. … . awakened with a big calcium imbalance reaction. Just starting to turn around now. Ugh!!! But God is noticeably close this time. Grateful! Very grateful. It's all so much easier to bear!

… OK so maybe didn't get back to sleep very much the rest of the night. Still in good spirits but if you wanted to pray that I could get some sort of catch up sleep this morning I sure would appreciate it! 💙

Would y'all please pray that I would sleep really well tonight? In the past six weeks since surgery every night includes 4 a.m. meds + food followed by two hours of sitting up in a recliner before laying down again. This plus the issues with back and thyroid balance has made me sleep deprived beyond words. Grateful for your prayers on my behalf! Thanks!

February 24 2014
What a feast of a day! Slept better last night and felt 'normal' all day.

Got to spend nice time with friends and family. Got to see my dog who is being cared for by my sister-in-law while I've been so sick. Haven't seen her since Christmas! And even got to stand up and share with the church family tonight. First time back at church since mid November! Wow!

Don't know if I will sleep tonight or if the clouds of difficulty will roll back in tomorrow. But so grateful for the feast that was today!

February 24, 2014
Went to bed at midnight and woke up at 3:30. No more sleep since then. This thyroid medication really keeps doing its number on me! This is the way it will be I guess until after treatment when they can begin to lower it some.

But on the bright side...how much more obvious it is that God over-ruled Saturday and Sunday. He GAVE me the special, good night of sleep on Saturday. He GAVE me such a wonderful day yesterday! He gave me that feast.

I can choose to be grumpy so that I don't sit at the feast again today. Or I can decide that I will be grateful that He is good and in charge.

By His grace, I will ask Him for help to have gratitude rather than grump.

February 24, 2014
OK so I officially am on the verge of collapsing. I've tried to sleep almost all day and maybe have fallen asleep twice for thirty minutes. I can hardly get out of bed now without feeling like I'm going to collapse. I have a call into my doctor to try to help me find a solution. Praying that we will find one and soon.

From God's Word:
John 14:27
Psalm 121

February 25, 2014
The doctor never responded to my call yesterday but the Great Physician heard mine.

I was able to sleep… Still woke up a number of times but able to fall back to sleep each time… Which is what I'm going to try to do now. It's like being given a half gallon of your favorite ice cream and a spoon and told to eat all you want! It feels so good to sleep!

I'm thanking God for overriding my messed up body and giving me some rest.

February 26, 2014
So this is practically unheard of! TWO nights in a row of something bordering on good sleep. I might even wind

up feeling human soon! I am so thankful for those who have been praying for me and to God for showing me His goodness not just by being in the middle of the storm clouds with me but by putting limits on them, too.

February 26 2014

Have been listening to a sermon and between that and the Thomas Watson book (All Things for the Good), my heart is getting a well-needed double whammy. So much to learn about truly loving God.

No wonder this trial is so big! God has so much work to do in my heart. I would love for it to end soon, but wouldn't be surprised if God really needs to keep workin …

I still will throw the biggest party ever when I get through this season. Ugh!!!! No fun! I do NOT like to suffer!

But I must say that I'm beginning to count it (almost) all joy that God has placed me in this trial to teach me and change me (James 1:2).

At very least it's getting easier to trace His hand of love in it.

February 28, 2014

I'm still continuing to sleep better! Not quite as superstar amazing as the first two days when I was at the collapsing point but still restorative. Also, my swallowing and calcium and thyroid levels all seem to be improving.

My 'fun' begins two weeks from Monday and I'm grateful that things seem to be getting a bit better across the board! Off to the endocrinologist for a final visit pre-treatment. Hopefully no surprises!

March 3, 2014

I broke the Guinness book of world record of sleep for me! Five nights in a row. Had a good doctor's appointment on Friday and she gave me the go ahead to travel down to Wintergreen this week. She said I can't stay up at the high altitude overnight but I can go for a few hours. Yay!

Best of all that means I might get to see my dear friends down in the valley over on Calf Mountain road for a short visit! How wonderful that will be if it all works out. It has been three months since I've last seen them!

Holding this trip loosely in my hand. It still may not happen if I take a dip for the worse.

In two weeks time my radiation treatment starts for two weeks.

I'm praying that I'll be held up physically and emotionally!

March 5, 2014

Today I'm thinking about Manna …

> The people of Israel ate the manna forty years, till they came to a habitable land. Exodus 16:35

Bread from heaven for thousands and thousands of people for forty years … wow! God has no problem with supplying what we need even though it looks impossibly big and we have no idea how He will do it!

> Now to Him who is able to do far more abundantly than all that we ask or think, according to the power at work within us, to him be glory in the church and in Christ Jesus. Ephesians 3:20, 21

This sounds like a promise of manna for our heart too. Each day ... whatever we need ... He will give us strength by His Holy Spirit. Really??? He can give more than I can think of or imagine? Wow! What encouragement to ask for more!

March 6, 2014
Looks like no trip down to Wintergreen for me! Here's why ...

Part of the preparation for my kind of radiation is a low iodine diet. Thyroid needs iodine so they take you off it for four weeks to make your cells really hungry for it. They then have you swallow radioactive iodine during treatment which the cells eagerly accept and are eventually killed by it. This is a bit like mice with peanut butter flavored poison. The hungrier they are the better it works.

So the diet is key to this treatment, but unfortunately I'm beginning to experience a whole new set of symptoms related to it. A change in altitude will only make things worse so it would be dumb for me to go. Treatment starts in a week and a half so I really need to try to do what's best.

I can hardly express how sad I am to not be going down to see my dear friends. It will be another three months now before I will be able to go. They are like a sweet piece of family and my heart aches to see them!

I need prayer in order to stay the course with this diet. I need to be grateful for the many good things that God is giving me even while He is withholding other things like seeing friends and a happy-feeling body.

For Christians, there are only two kinds of days... Good days and good fighting days.

Everyone knows what a good day is. But a good fighting day is one which may not look immediately good on the surface. However, because we know that God is in it, working for our good and His glory, we can fight in our hearts to rejoice in it. A good fighting day is as good and often even a better gift than the regular kind of good day.

Off to battle…but right now fighting back the tears!!!

March 8, 2014

Spent a lot of time this morning thinking about all I have to thank God for. It was like drinking out of a fire hydrant!

I could hardly stop and take proper notice of all the ways He's shown His kindness to me especially in the last few months!

So many dear friends are a big part of how He has done this. No one should be treated with as much care as I have! I am speechless from the overflowing show of His and their love.

March 8, 2014

Oh, what fun! Our little mountain band got together out on the parking lot and played some Bluegrass favorites and soaked in the sun! So great to hit the hammered dulcimer again and enjoy the promise of spring!

March 10, 2014

Getting the jitters as I think about the unknowns of next week. Reminding myself that they are neither unknown or unruly to God…and He loves me!!!

Word of Wisdom:

Jesus, I My Cross Have Taken

I have called Thee 'Abba, Father',
I have set my heart on Thee;
Storms may howl, and clouds may gather,
All must work for good to me.

Words by HENRY F. LYTE 1793-1847

March 10, 2014

Word of Wisdom:

God calls us to imagine that the best possible future
lies in the path God chooses instead of the path of our
desires. – THABITI ANYABWILE

Like a river glorious, is God's perfect peace,
Over all victorious, in its bright increase;
Perfect, yet it floweth, fuller every day,
Perfect, yet it groweth, deeper all the way.

Hidden in the hollow of His blessed hand,
Never foe can follow, never traitor stand;
Not a surge of worry, not a shade of care,
Not a blast of hurry touch the spirit there.

Every joy or trial falleth from above,
Traced upon our dial by the Sun of Love;
We may trust Him fully all for us to do.
They who trust Him wholly find Him wholly true.

Stayed upon Jehovah, hearts are fully blest
Finding, as He promised, perfect peace and rest.

FRANCES R. HAVERGAL 1876

March 12, 2014

We are coming down to the big fight now...

#1   the iodine diet is really wreaking havoc on me, especially messing with my emotions.

#2 I'm going to be given four injections of 'special sauce' ... Two before each radioactive capsule. They can make some people very sick and typically I'm one of those kinds. There can be some crazy stuff that can happen too and I'd really choose sick over the dangerous side effects.

#3   the radioactive treatment itself ... Again it can make you very sick and it can have some nasty side effects. This is usually temporary but can even be permanent especially to the tear ducts and salivary glands. I will have one capsule next Wednesday and one next Thursday.

#4   After each capsule there is a scan to show where the cancer is. So time for the unveiling of what's what. As you can imagine that feels like good news and bad news.

#5   I'm so spiritually and mentally and physically weary. I am in such need of prayer to be resting in God's good plans and in His ability to do exactly what He knows is best.

March 12, 2014

Once more it's amazing how God has answered prayers!!!

So grateful for the better day, for everyone who prayed, and of course for God!!!

This is definitely about asking for new mercies each day like the Israelites gathering the manna each day that God provided them with in the wilderness.

What's hard is that I feel like I'm a lame lady stuck in the tent and must depend not just on God to rain down new manna 'mercies' each day, but also on the efforts of others. God is calling me to sit tight and out of my helplessness depend more than ever upon the efforts of others to gather and bring to me what I need.

Perhaps God puts us in these situations to remind us that when we lay down our lives for each other in this very un-worldly way, we more clearly show that He is alive and His love (lived out in us) is wonderful.

But I definitely chafe a bit at being so very needy so very often.

March 14, 2014

Reading in John 4 this morning about hungry and tired Jesus waiting by the well in Samaria while the disciples go to town for food.

While they are gone, the 'sleazy' Samaritan woman comes. Jesus and she have the amazing conversation that leads to her salvation and totally changes her life.

The disciples come back with food, but Jesus tells them that He's satisfied already. With what? Doing the will of His Father … in the form of rescuing a cast-off woman like this! Wow!

Think! We have a Savior who so delights to save us that this satisfies Him more than meeting His body's basic needs! And didn't He do this most of all on the cross… sacrificed His needs for ours?

Oh, to remember these things and live to honor Him accordingly! Whatever He asks of me next week in my treatments, I hope I can reflect Him and my gratitude for His love towards me. I am as equally undeserving as the woman at the well.

March 17, 2014

4:50 a.m. ... can't get back to sleep. My heart just won't be settled. Visions of side effects are dancing in my head when I'm really wanting it to be sugar plums dancing there instead. This is definitely NOT the night before Christmas in my heart!

Or is it? There's a dead rat in my heart somewhere, to use a D.C. analogy. Rats die in weird places in this city. You can smell them but can't quite get to them.

That's how my heart feels. There's a lie or maybe a whole family of lies rotting someplace in my heart's recesses; Things it refuses to believe about God and His goodness; what I'm going through and what He has planned ahead. Then there are the things God has in mind to do that frankly I'd rather just do without ... and it stinks.

But maybe it is the night before Christmas after all ... it's just that I'm getting a service call from pest management in my stocking.

I'm tired of the smell that this lie has been making but somehow I've been happier to live with it than go through prying open the floorboards of my heart to find it and get rid of it.

Perhaps God is using this trial to make me hate the stench of this lie so much that I'm happy for the demolition needed to be rid of it. That sure does sound like our great big good God!

So it's ugh!!!! But somehow also 'praise God!'

Perhaps, just perhaps, this will turn out to be not just one of the hardest seasons of my life but also one of best presents I've received.

God is so good and patient with me!

From God's Word:
Isaiah 25:8-9

That soul though all hell should endeavor to shake, I'll never, no never, no never forsake!

GEORGE KEITH 1639-1716

Psalm 91:4

Every millisecond of your misery in the path of obedience is producing a peculiar glory you will get because of that.

A Song for the Suffering – JOHN PIPER

March 17, 2014
Made it to hospital!!!!

March 17, 2014
Blood work and first injection done. I'm back home! A little nausea and headache kicking in but not too bad. The nurse says that usually what you've got in the three hours after the injection is how it's going to affect you. One hour down …

I met a nice lady about fifteen years older than me who will be doing almost the same schedule as me. It's nice to have a partner.

March 17, 2014

Prayers were absolutely answered! Fought the nausea headache most of the day. Thought I was going to lose a few times but then the worst passed.

I go back tomorrow for round two. I think it's supposed to make me more tired and probably sick again but who knows right?

I was grateful that it went as well as it did!

Tip from a friend: Ginger Tea made by shaving off some real ginger root into boiling water and steeping for several minutes and sweetened with honey might help the nausea.

March 18, 2014

I am so thankful to God for all who have been praying as I go through my two weeks of treatment!

I had my second injection today. These shots change hormone levels rapidly to make my cancer cells take up more radioactive iodine.

They certainly are working now. Felt pretty good until this evening. Fever chills, aches and very very tired today. Some people get this. Not much nausea though. Yay for that!

Tomorrow at 10:30 I have my first actual radiation capsule. So we will see how that goes. I and others are praying that it works well and that I tolerate it.

Thursday will be my first full body scan. I should have more news of what's what then. May I rest in God and know that His resources will be enough to bring me through whatever lies ahead.

I am so glad that He is such a good Father who understands my ins and outs, ups and downs. It's all too much for me to figure out what will be ahead and what I will have to cope with. Time to just relinquish everything and rest in His embrace of me and the situation.

From God's Word:
ISAIAH 41:10

March 19, 2014
What a night of insight this has been! Today I was particularly missing a number of the people, places and things that have been removed during this season.

I miss gluten, my family, my dog, my viola and cello, my friends down near Wintergreen, and the mountains down there too…as well as an optimistic feel about what's around the corner to name a few things!

But, as I was thinking about these things so fondly, I was struck by how none of them hold a candle to all the Lord has been and done for me and even promises me for the future.

There's such a contrast in how untrusting, ungrateful and forgetful I can be of Him while at the same time so full of sparkle and joy over these delightful but much smaller things.

How shamefully out of order things are in my heart! I need to drop my focus on what I cherish but can't have and switch it to greater gratitude for God!

I wonder if I've just discovered a leading member of the dead rat society that's been stinking things up in my heart.

From God's Word:
JOHN 15: 5-9

March 19, 2014

Back from hospital. Ten lovely radioactive capsules downed. This is the tiny dose! Would love to not throw up!!!

Waiting one more hour then going to enjoy some nice hot paleo gluten free rolls with some egg white avocado stuff. That is actually not bad at least for another week while I continue this diet.

Scans are tomorrow at 9:30 a.m. for three hours then I get the first results of where the cancer is. If there are no surprises then we will have a victory dinner tomorrow night.

Otherwise …. There will be news to get adjusted to and grace to ask for.

> *Word of Wisdom:*
> Thou has disarmed me of the means in which I trusted and I have no strength but in thee.
>
> *Valley of Vision, Grace in Trials.*

March 20, 2014

Good morning, everyone! Off to scan #1 soon. Then I'll hear the first results.

Results they hope they will find … Only cancer in neck near where thyroid is.

Common places where thyroid cancer likes to go afterwards …

Lungs (favorite location), brain, spine and bone, according to my doctor. They can go other places.

I'm having to 'rope in the little doggies' in my mind as I wait for results. Some of those places I'd especially prefer not to have to deal with.

It's fine if I feel 'penniless' and unable to deal with results because God Himself will provide what is needed.

March 20, 2014

After a big scare and an extra scan they ruled out cancer in the esophagus and believe it is only in the neck where they thought it would be.

Apparently I have weird extra partially formed thyroid cells leftover from my days in the womb before my thyroid fully formed. They are hanging out near the esophagus in the wrong place. That's what lit up like cancer.

I am officially weird.

It has been an emotional day of waiting, panicking a bit, then being relieved.

Just a bit of blood work to go then home to a celebratory dinner.

March 20, 2014

Is this added sweetness or what! My next door neighbor offered to make me filet mignon for dinner! I was just going to be happy with some sort of iodine free but boring con-coction. Yum!

March 26, 2014

Well, the big event is tomorrow.

I wish I could say I'm bravely facing it but I'm just plain scared and maybe a bit depressed.

Have a million things to do but just can't get up to do them.

I'm praying for:

The Lord to give me courage!

The lemon drops not to inflame my very tender esophagus too much and do what they are supposed to do in protecting my salivary glands

The nausea not to be too bad. (The low dose last week brought me close to vomiting and this one will be much bigger)

The meds to be effective.

Me to cope with loneliness as the two weeks I'll be away from everyone.

Me to trust that whatever side effects do come will be bearable because God will keep them within the bounds He knows best for me.

Here's the schedule:

Get admitted tomorrow at 11 a.m., then receive dose around 1 p.m. In seclusion at hospital through Friday when my radiation levels are down enough to be released from my special room.

Then home and under special haz mat conditions.

March 27, 2014

I can't believe it but I have some cell phone service in here!

Took capsule at 2:30 p.m. They brought in a little machine that registers my radiation level.

I've waited two hours and now the game begins. I have just started the lemon drops and drinking like a fish every ten minutes.

So many showers! Everything scrubbed and washed – including the tongue!!! – every two hours. All these things get the radiation out of me.

Tomorrow morning they will bring the little machine back and see how well I've done in getting down my levels. Right now I'm at thirteen whatever that means.

I can be released as soon as its low enough.

They gave me anti-nausea meds and, so far, so good. The lemon drops are already hurting my esophagus a bit but oh well … .

From God's Word:

PSALM 34:4

I sought the Lord and He answered me, and delivered me from all my fears.

March 27, 2014

Things are basically going well. I look like a drowned rat from all the showers but that's ok.

But the pain in my esophagus is already starting to get intense and i have a good 120 more lemon drops to go over the next thirteen hours.

I need prayer.

March 28, 2014

God is obviously answering people's prayers!

I have gone from looking like a drowned rat to something like the cat dragged in and often close to throwing up. I won't be posting a selfie anytime soon - that's for sure!!!

BUT esophagitis hasn't gotten worse and I've been able to keep up the lemon drops.

But NEVER EVER want to have them or Blue Gatorade again!

9:30 a.m. radiation readings are drawing closer. Hopefully will get to go home this morning.

March 28, 2014

Passed radiation test! It's down from thirteen to 3.4 whatever that means. Feel quite sick but at least I can stop the lemon drops now. Hopefully be ready to go home in an hour! Yay!

March 28, 2014

I'm at home resting. I do have to keep up the lemon drops for another day but many less per hour. Nausea is much better! Starting to get some pain in the neck and salivary gland area that is related to the treatment but very bearable at this point. Grateful.

The weirdest thing is knowing that the radiation I'm giving off is at a level that is harmful to others if they are too close for too long but I don't feel anything radiating from my body.

I have to take multiple showers a day, flush toilet twice, use a separate bathroom, use disposable plates, cover surfaces to avoid the sweat from my hands being left on things that others use etc. but I don't feel a thing.

This is like a weird illustration of faith. You believe and live in the certainty of something being there even though you can't see it.

March 29, 2014

I slept eleven hours last night! Can't believe it! I'm still tired but I guess I did just give my body quite a work out!

Hopefully it will now be eight weeks of healing as my blood count and bone marrow gets roasted and then comes back up into normal range … .

And hopefully the prize at the end will be getting to go to Wintergreen up in those blue ridge mountains and even more, down in the valley, seeing friends in early June.

> *From God's Word:*
> COLOSSIANS 2:6-7
> COLOSSIANS 3:15-17

March 29, 2014

While I'm at it it's interesting reading in John 9 about the man born blind.

The disciples ask if it was the man or his parent's sin that caused this condition. Jesus tells them, 'It was not that this man sinned, nor his parents, but that the works of God might just be displayed in him. We must work the works of him who sent me while it is day…'

What Jesus did FOR the man was just the beginning of what He would do THROUGH the man.

The same God who planned for this illness to be healed as a good work of Jesus, chose to equip this blind man with a courageous heart and a golden tongue. Unlike his parents, he spoke up about Jesus and spoke out against the false accusations against Jesus.

So God's glory wasn't just displayed in Jesus' miracle but in the work that God prepared for the man to do after Jesus had healed him.

It's like a time release capsule that keeps on displaying God's glory – here I am talking about it over 2,000 years later!

A good word of encouragement is that God changes us in His work in us, but also equips us to display Him in response to that work.

God has equipped us to be a display of Him as a result of His work in us!

What display of God's glory will our response to His work in us be today?

March 30, 2014

I've started developing pain in upper right abdominal area that finally has gotten bad enough for me to call the doctor. He thinks it's probably my gall bladder. He said I can wait a few more hours but if things get worse I need to go in for blood work and maybe to have it removed.

This is so discouraging! Please pray that God would choose to heal this and I would not have to face surgery now. Or, if it is to be that He would help me be cheerful and my body will cope with it well.

March 30, 2014

Still at home guzzling clear liquids and hoping this will pass …

Just read this …

> The Lord knows how to order things better than I. The Lord sees further than I do; I only see things at present but the Lord sees a great while from now. And how do I know that had it not been for this affliction, I should have been undone. I know that the love of God may as well stand with afflicted condition as with a prosperous condition.
>
> Jeremiah Burroughs

Praying that I live this even now! He is worthy of it!

March 31, 2014
Update … . Blue Gatorade is officially reinstated as my friend. It got me through the night. Pain is much decreased but still there a bit. Ugh!!!

So … Just put a call into my doctor's office so they can call me and give me next step advice. Still being under quarantine from the radioactive iodine certainly complicates things a bit. Plus, tomorrow is my big scheduled scan that's supposed to be the grand finale to the radiation treatment. Hmmmm … don't know how all this works out.

March 31, 2014
Thankful for God's answer to prayer. I continue to improve. Doctor and I have decided to wait until I finish my quarantine period to pursue what's going on further. Hopefully, everything will stay settled.

April 1, 2014
Off to the grand finale scan on my own! Three hours of fun but this one should give them the best picture they can have of exactly where the cancer is. I didn't want Mark to be too close with me as I'm still somewhat radioactive so I'm doing this one by myself. May God sustain me whatever the result.

April 1, 2014
The grand finale isn't going quite as expected. Please pray for me.

They had to do one extra scan of my hip area and now I have to wait another two hours for another camera for another look. They are concerned that they may be seeing cancer in my hips in a couple places.

The good news is that these spots lit up. That means they took in the radioactive iodine which hopefully will kill it.

The bad news...well I guess you can understand that this makes my cancer stage four and it has spread to the last place it typically spreads.

I'm not doing very well right now. Praying that I live out what I believe.

Here I sit editing Sunday school curriculum on what concept? God's people know heaven is their home.

God will not let us preach what we do not live ourselves. Ligon Duncan.

May I mourn but not as those with no hope. I have so much hope!!!

April 1, 2014

OK praise God! The hips are clear of cancer! It was other stuff that took in the iodine but will dissipate eventually!

There were some bits in the neck but that was expected.

What a relief!

Next step will be a repeat of this radioactive iodine (but a lower dose) in a year to see if they got everything.

I have been helped through this very, very difficult day.

April 4, 2014

Today marks a happy reunion! My cello and me! It's been months since I've been well enough to consider playing.

Thank You, God, for letting me once more have this pleasure!

April 5, 2014

I feel like I've been given a new beginning. Just realized that it's been eleven months since first my back then all sorts of illness struck then eventually ended up with the cancer.

God has given me this new start. How does He want me to re-build as I go forward? What have I learned? What does He really want me to do? What should be different?

Excited but also wary that I don't just forget all He's taught me.

April 6, 2014

I think Rose Marie Miller summed up how we should love each other so well in her new book *Nothing Is impossible with God*.

She talks about asking God to enlarge our hearts so that we love a broken world more than our own comfort.

How many times am I tempted to not do something or say something for someone else because I'm concerned that their needs might be overwhelming or their response might be hurtful?

The Apostle John tells us what Jesus said when He faced the cross (which was both overwhelming and hurtful):

'Now is my soul troubled. And what shall I say? "Father save me from this hour?" But for this purpose I have come to this hour. Father, glorify your name.'

Oh, Lord, help me love like you! Loving others and You like Jesus did. Counting the cost and going ahead. Holding nothing back.

April 7, 2014

But Jesus would not entrust Himself to them, for he knew all people. John 2:24

Jesus loved us like none other, yet He withheld the feeding of His heart, the value of His worth and the direction of His path.

My life can be littered with a desire for the approval of others. How many times do I seize up with the fear of what 'they' will think!

That's when I realize that it's not just 'they' that are the root of the issue; it's what I do with 'they.' It's me!!!

I think the word for that is pride. Ugh!!!

It's a terrible but freeing moment when you realize that there is something you can do if you tend to care too much about the opinions of others like I do … think less about yourself!

Oh, to be realistic and accepting of my own strengths and weaknesses! Oh, to entrust my heart and my life to God!

Easier said than done!

Word of Wisdom:

When God purposes to build, He seeks for a ruin. When He plans to plant a garden, He starts in the desert PATRICIA ST JOHN

Let us not settle with prayerlessness and so settle for powerlessness. DAVID PLATT

April 11, 2014

Just past midnight! Just turned April 11th! I am officially out of radiation quarantine! Yahoo!

I guess this really means I'm on the other side of the active phase of my bout with thyroid cancer at least for now!

Looking forward to hugging people and hitting the swimming pool today!

Ahhhh!!!

April 12, 2014

> No eye has seen, no ear has heard, no heart has
> imagined, what God has prepared for those who
> love him. 1 CORINTHIANS 2:9-12

If cherry blossoms are any kind of appetizer of the beauties God has cooked up, I can't imagine what the feast will be like!

April 12, 2014

I'm needing prayer again. I think I'm starting to hit some increasingly bumpy side effects. It's like my whole digestive tract is raw ... which it might be since the radiation is both absorbed and flows all the way through it.

I was told that different side effects can take weeks or months to hit. I'm guessing this must be the first of mine.

I need wisdom to know what to do about the nausea and pain.

I guess I will have to hold days of feeling good a bit more loosely.

April 14, 2014

Update ... Still so, so sick! I'm grateful though to have had a little break earlier today to get my taxes printed off and ready to go. Then whoosh back it came.

And thankful for a little book called a *Cluster of Camphor* by Mrs C. H. Spurgeon. She wrote these meditations in the midst of sickness. There's one in which she even stops writing because she suddenly becomes so ill.

It was one about our times being in God's hands. When she finishes writing the meditation (apparently weeks later) she mentions how much easier it was to write the meditation than live it out as God called her to, right in the middle of it.

So true!!! I'm trying to remember what God and Mrs Spurgeon both point to: that He really does have my times in His hands.

It's amazing to think of how many thousands of lives the Lord has blessed by putting a megaphone up to that woman's honest sufferings. She certainly has been a huge blessing to me.

Over a hundred years later the Lord continues NOT to have wasted that lady's sorrows.

It gives me hope that He's not wasting mine either.

So ... Don't know how much sleep I'm going to get tonight, but I'm going to try to be joyful somehow anyway.

Word of Wisdom:

BEHOLD THE LIGHT OF CANDLE FOUR:
What we have lost God will restore
When He is finished with His art,
The silent worship of our heart.
When God creates a humble hush,
And makes Leviathan His brush,
It won't be long until the rod
Becomes the tender kiss of God.
JOHN PIPER

April 18, 2014

For the first time in my life, I've woken up on Good Friday morning and I feel the same excitement as I do on Christmas morning, right before everyone gets up and I know we will go downstairs to the Christmas tree and the presents and the celebration of the day.

What a gift I was given this day, 2,000 years ago! It trumps all my fears. Jesus bore all the wrath of God on the cross for me while I was still His enemy. There is nothing that He cannot take care of! He is faithful!

> He who did not spare His own Son but freely
> gave Him up for us, will He not along with Him,
> graciously give us all things? ROMANS 8:32

There has never been such a love as this!!!!

Life's journey will be along dark mountains that feel too difficult to cross and green easy valleys where I will be lazy and forgetful. But He has been faithful and will ALWAYS be found faithful. The road is not the point, the Guide is!

> Come let us worship and bow down before our Maker
> … let the whole earth stand in awe. PSALM 95:6

Good, good, Good Friday! Good, good, good season of suffering that has brought me this joy to my heart!

Does He not do all things well?

April 19 – Psalm 30

April 20, 2014

> *Word of Wisdom:*
> Most people want acutely something that cannot be
> had in this world. We reduce all of life to a personal

comfort and pleasure delivery system. We pack into this life all the pleasure, happiness and excitement we can. We ask people, places and things to satisfy our soul and redeem our past but they can't. We require a broken world to make us happy but it can't and never will.

When we ask 'now' to give us only what eternity can, we wind up driven, frustrated, discouraged, and ultimately hopeless. We live with a destination mentality instead of a preparation mentality.

This world with all its present joys and sorrows is not our final address. Our complete, personal happiness is not what God is working on in the here and now, because the plan of His grace is to deliver us out of this world to one that is much much better.

Forever by PAUL DAVID TRIPP

April 22, 2014

One of the biggest things I think I've learned about myself through these months is how much I love to dodge difficulty. I find plenty of good things to do, but leave some things undone that God would have me do. Why? Because I'm quite aware of how hard they would be for me to do.

This thyroid cancer treatment was something that has been way too big for me to handle on my own but it was a road I could not escape. It has been hard in ways that I was afraid it was going to be, but I still had to press through it with the help of God and others.

Now, I'm asking God for the courage to face head on other things that seem way too big for me to handle (spiritual heart issues) It's time to tackle them. I need to choose the difficulties in hope of gaining changes. Only by God's grace will this come to pass!

April 29, 2014

So on the down side, I'm starting to hit the salivary gland side effects from the radiation. Dry mouth: It's hard to eat without those little critters working. This also seems to be messing with my esophagus and stomach because things don't get a good start digesting in the mouth as they should. So that's pretty ugh! However, this should pass in a few weeks or months hopefully.

On the very up side, God has begun to give me a joy like I've never had before. Resting in Him and knowing that His plans will win are helping me to let go of the things I stress out about.

I'm not saying I don't leap toward anxiety anymore. I do and think I always will. It's part of my make-up.

But as I've been spending so much more time meditating on the truths of His promised victory it's beginning to show up as the fruit of joy.

And by joy I mean a contentedness that doesn't come from what I'm going through but from the good God who is taking me through it.

So while I love, love, love to feel good and look forward to days where my body is not hurting, I am very, very grateful for this path. God chose it for me. He was right and was good to use it as He has.

And I am so grateful to be His child!

April 30, 2014

I would so appreciate your prayers. The pain from the side effects is growing and seems to have kicked up whatever is the issue with the heartburn/stomach portion of me to a new intensity. I need wisdom to know what to do and to find relief.

April 30, 2014

Romans 8:28-29 'And we know that for those who love God all things work together for good for those who are called according to his purpose ... to be conformed to likeness of His Son.'

All things for the good ... For those who love God ... His purposes ... Into the likeness of His Son.

The future. Instead of worrying that the worst outcome is in the works, it's far more appropriate to imagine the best outcome I can... and then know that if God does not bring that, it is only because He has replaced it with something I need even more to complete His work to make me into the likeness of His Son.

So ... What comes may be something that looks (and even is) terrible on face value. But my heart can take joy because my Heavenly Father has given me something BETTER than I can imagine, planned with His long-sighted, perfect view.

He's replacing my best guess with His best!

What a privilege to live as God's child and under this promise! Oh, to be still and know that He is God! Oh, to adopt His clear vision for my blindness and run in delight to His will.

This doesn't take the pain or the trouble away, but re-values it from something that feels broken to something that is of greater worth than gold.

May 2, 2014

Last night I was so weary of persevering through this battle with illness. Tired of taking joy in being shaped through affliction. Tired of fighting fears and anxiousness. Tired of waiting and wondering if it will end soon or at all.

But then last night I spoke with a friend who shared about a long trial she's facing and how the sweetest part came at the very end.

That helped me hold on for the gift that might be just ready to be 'delivered' today that couldn't be delivered yesterday because it wasn't the right time yet.

The end of this trial seems long overdue, but what do I really know? Very, very little!

God's Word tells us that our Heavenly Father knows how to give good gifts to His children far better than we do … And I'm a pretty good gift giver, so that's encouraging!

So it's back to making lemonade out of what feels like lemons … and doing it cheerfully … well at least pretty much!

From God's Word:
ISAIAH 55: 8-11
ISAIAH 41: 8 -14

May 3, 2014
Today was a day of gratefulness because I'm feeling better. Absolutely. But also, because these past few months have helped me to stop and savor many small goodnesses that my filter usually let's go by. Why? Because usually I'm hurrying on my way to the next thing.

For instance: the sound of birds chirping, the smell of the flowers on the spring breeze, my dog sitting with her paws crossed here next to me on the front steps as I'm eating soup a friend made and listening to my husband's crazy combination of music in the background. What a sweet day! I want to relish it. Simple pleasures all, but what a feast!

May 7, 2014

Oh how I need prayer and support for all this health stuff! The various things I am experiencing keep growing and I have a doctor's appointment at 10:30 today. I need her to have wisdom and for me to release all of this to God and rest in Him. My, this is hard! I am so thankful for all those people persevering with me.

May 10, 2014

If you have never heard of *Cheque Book of the Bank of Faith* by C. H. Spurgeon, you are missing a real treat! It is maybe his best set of little devotions. Each day is a promise from God that is described wonderfully.

But perhaps the best part of the book is the preface. He tells you how to use these promises ... and really every truth we learn about God.

He reminds us that It's not enough to just read over a promise or truth once. It takes effort and meditation to make truth .... well ... truly true to you.

So much of my current trial has been learning that my soul has been like a room, with the truths of scripture lying like a roll of wallpaper on a table – the protective plastic wrapping still on.

It's in the room where it's supposed to go, but please, some-one get that plastic off, cut it into pieces and start putting it up in place!

God has used the agony of my fears to be the incentive I needed to flee to the truths of His Word ... and (begin to) learn how to make them truly true to me.

It has taken a lot of effort but I have had to go get one truth after another up on my heart's wall. I've had to keep on staring at them so that they become the comfort they were always able to be.

I understand more than ever Paul's language of disciplining oneself for the race of life. It will not happen without effort.

Good thing God Himself refuses to leave us as the couch potatoes we like to be, and gets us up and moving on towards Him.

He is so good and wise!

> *Word of Wisdom:*
> We cannot be too much of children with our
> heavenly father. Our young ones ask no question
> about our will or our power, but having once received
> a promise from father, they rejoice in the prospect
> of its fulfillment, never doubting that it is sure as
> the sun. May many readers, whom I may never see,
> discover the duty and delight of such childlike trust
> in God as they are reading the little bit which I have
> prepared for each day in the year.
>
> C. H. SPURGEON, *Cheque Book of the Bank of Faith*

May 13, 2014

> You shall not curse the people for they are blessed.
>
> NUMBERS 22:12

Balaam was being paid by the terrified king of Moab to curse the Israelites. He was certain the Israelites would take over their land. But all the money or enemies in the world could not have their way. The Lord forbid Balaam to curse the people. It was not His will so it simply would not, could not happen. These were a blessed people. These were His people! No evil would come upon them.

Isn't that wonderful! The Lord stands as a perfect, strong protector for His people and His good plans for them will not be broken.

May 15, 2014

OK so if you've been following me on this journey you might have noticed that I've been changing. It's true! And it is His doing!

I have a long way to go, but I know joy that I've never known before. And found God's Word and His Holy Spirit working inside me to be powerful to bring changes that I never thought possible. Fear that has been my master and bound me in many ways really has met its match.

I felt fear would always rule over me. I see that it will be my lifetime foe who comes back most every day to challenge me. It will always be too strong just for me, *but* when I go to God and use His weapons, (Not just know about His weapons, but really USE them daily!!!!) He will do it! If you are feeling that there will never be a change in your life, take hope! God has been truly able to change me some already and I have hope that He can continue to change me. He can and will help you, too, with whatever is your struggle! What an able God we have! His Word and His Spirit are powerful to change us.

May 15, 2014

The more I see of the struggles of this world and the flimsy, ineffective solutions that it offers, the more grateful I am to go to Jesus and the deep, eternal, all mighty power and hope found in Him.

The storms may rage but He rules them all. Often He doesn't take them away but harnesses their fury to be the power that helps us sail home.

I can say with full confidence now ... I would take one day in His peaceful courts or in His fiery furnace than a thousand elsewhere.

He is the good shepherd! He knows what He's doing! If I can encourage you in anything it is to run to Him and find what you truly need and are searching for in Him. It WILL be found there!

Why is it that this bitterest pill I've had to swallow is bringing the sweetest healing I've ever known? And this miracle comes only through the work of the Great Physician who not only heals the sick but raises the dead of heart and of body. Nothing is impossible for Him even if it is impossible for man.

Taste and see that The Lord is good!!

May 17, 2014

> *Words of Wisdom:*
> from Corrie ten Boom
>
> Man's importunity is God's opportunity. He uses our problems as building materials for His miracles.
>
> CORRIE TEN BOOM, *Tramp for The Lord*

Corrie's sister Betsie had a plan for taking the gospel to many places, including Germany after the war.

'To all the world? But that will take much money,' Corrie replied.

'Yes, but God will provide,' Betsy said. 'We must do nothing else to bring the gospel and He will take care of us. After all, He owns the cattle on a thousand hills. If we need money we will just ask the father to sell a few cows.'

I love this childlike faith!

May 18, 2014

When I look at all that God has made and how perfectly He has made each thing to be suited to what it is to do, it encourages me that He has also created His people to be suited for what He has in mind for them to do.

What bird has no wings that was meant to fly? What fish lacks the fins and gills to swim? Surely He has also equipped us for whatever particular life He has called us to. With His grace, He will make sure of that!

May 26, 2014

> Who shall separate us from the love of Christ? Shall tribulation, or distress, or persecution, or famine, or nakedness, or dangerous, or swords? ... No, and all these things we are more than conquerors through him who loved us. For I am sure that neither life nor death, nor angels nor rulers, nor things present nor things to come, nor powers, nor height nor depth, nor anything else in all creation, will be able to separate us from the love of God in Christ Jesus our Lord.
>
> ROMANS 8:35,37-39

Sometimes I mistakenly think that God's love is like mine. My love can be little more than a changeable feeling. Or, I may love someone deeply and steadfastly, but still my love is often powerless to deliver what is needed to those I love.

God's love is not just a feeling. It is not changeable or weak. It is intense, steadfast and completely powerful to deliver what He knows is most needful to those He loves. Just look what His love did on the cross!

Nothing can separate us from God's love in Christ. This is a big deal! It means nothing will be able to separate us from what God knows is best for us and He will bring it to completion. That makes all the things we fear most powerless to injure us. Thank you, God!

May 27, 2014
God in His wisdom and love does not always change the circumstances we face, but He promises to always change us to meet them, to be with us through them, and to bless us through them.

It is not always the solution we are looking for at the time, but far better in the end.

> *From God's Word:*
> 2 CORINTHIANS 4:17-18

May 28, 2014
I am increasingly convinced that the harder the thing God allows in His children's life, the greater the blessing.

I still prefer the gifts with the bright bows and cheerful wrappings. I still dread the ones wrapped in black and greys, but He has yet to show anything but goodness and kindness in these that He's chosen.

Take courage, any of you out there struggling today! Taste and see that the Lord is good! Oh, so good.

May 29, 2014

I am thinking (and feeling!) the difference between God giving us grace to make it through each day and God giving us grace that makes actual changes in us.

The first is like Him providing us with our daily bread.

The second is building upon the foundation of our salvation.

The first is immediate, but short-lived, need after need. The second is transformation. He delights to give both and we need both.

I've been living lopsidedly on the daily need kind of God's grace. These big trials that God has kindly given me have shown me how much I need this second kind of grace for life's storms not to flatten me.

I'm learning to be grateful for the trials that come and excited for the things God wants to teach me. His grace will help me to really learn them and live by them…at least a bit more.

> *From God's Word:*
> PSALM 20

May 31, 2014

What a lot of fighting fear the last few days have been! Fear over what? Oh just about anything imaginable!

It's amazing how victory comes one day then the next day all the territory I gained seems to be have been lost. Yet ... half the victory is being willing to struggle. And that I've been doing!

While I feel very sad to have not sent fear running away with God's truth as I would have liked, His truth is still true! And there is forgiveness wider than the ocean and love higher than the heavens for me.

I can sit defeated and sad or I can praise God all the more that He would love someone like me!

So up I get, going forward in His grace. What a wonderful God we have!

From God's Word:
2 CORINTHIANS 4:10

June 3, 2014
I'm asking my faithful praying friends to pray that my thyroid levels stabilize and the side effects of muscle spasms and anxiety subside.

On Thursday my levels were off the chart so they have now reduced my Meds. However, it will take a while for my body to see the difference.

The anxiousness is incredible and there now seems to be quite a hole in my esophagus/stomach area that they are treating as an ulcer.

I basically need to be as calm and un-worrying as possible to heal it while the thyroid imbalance makes me anxious at the drop of a hat. It is crazy!!!

I'm spending a few days at the beach so I pray that these would be calming and The Lord would heal body, mind and spirit. The ocean sure is a wonderful help.

June 3, 2014

I seem to be having some improvement this afternoon for the first time in almost a week! Anxiety has come down and stomach pain a bit better too. Felt good enough to even go out to dinner and eat normally. Grateful!

June 7, 2014

> Consider what you might add to the gospel. Life is
> found in God + _____. ED WELCH

How freeing to know while there may be a whole stack of things we put in that blank, none of them are needed!

Every single one of the things I put in that blank have chains attached to them and leave me in bondage! Not one of them are needed for my salvation thanks to Christ.

Ah freedom!!! How amazing is God's grace!!

June 13, 2014

> God is not a man that he should lie, nor a son of
> man that he should change his mind. Does he
> speak and then not act? Does he promise and not
> fulfill? NUMBERS 23:19

What promises of God are you forgetting to take comfort in today, knowing that He will fulfill them?

June 13, 2014

I have been thinking a lot about how much I love the control of knowing what's coming next...especially HOW God will provide for me next. I like predictable and easily identifiable means. Meaning: I love to walk by sight!!!

But then I've been thinking about how kind it is that God doesn't just supply what we need but always supplies it in the way we need it.

In the wilderness God gave the Israelites their food on a daily basis only. He used miraculous means to humble them and to teach them that they do not live by bread but by Him. And He did this for year upon year because like me, they loved to walk by sight, they did not depend on Him or walk by faith!

God could have given them food in many ways during those forty years, but His means and methods are as carefully and lovingly chosen as the things He actually provides. And who's to say which is actually the more important gift?

In my case, I know I need the training through the method of God's choice every bit as much as I need the original thing I asked Him to provide!

June 22, 2014
Just a little update! I'm doing better. Made my first trips down to Wintergreen on my own and stayed for a few days! Still have some issues related to thyroid levels getting adjusted but they are less frequent. Mid July will be the first blood tests to check if the cancer is growing…. that lurks in the back of my mind.

Mark is on sabbatical through July and we are hoping for some good resting and healing time together after this crazy ride. I think we both are very tired.

June 22, 2014
Whoever has my commands and keeps them is the one who loves me. The one who loves me will be loved

by my Father, and I too will love them and show
myself to them. JOHN 14:21

Much of the Christian life is about relinquishing living life
on your terms and instead with God's help, moving bit by
bit, day by day, to living life on His terms.

So the fight goes on to not just KNOW God's good commands but OBEY them and desire His rule over our lives.

Not only is this what He calls us to do, if we are His
people, but it is best and it is blessed!

Best ... Because He is wiser than us. He is always right,
even when His mysterious ways seem all wrong.

And blessed ... because He blesses us with more of His
presence as we obey Him.

June 30, 2014
Sometimes I think I live a museum life with God. I read
His great works, His amazing promises and believe they
are true, but I leave them behind glass to gaze at and treat
almost like they are part of a past way of how God's worked
among His people.

Today is a 'Break glass in case of emergency' day! I need
to take hold of these truths again and put them to use. They
belong in my tool box not in my display cabinet if they are
to make a difference in my life.

> *Words of Wisdom:*
> Truths are often delivered to us, like wheat in full
> ears, to the end we should rub them out before we eat
> them, and take pains about them, before we have the
> comfort of them. JOHN BUNYAN, *All Loves Excelling*

July 12, 2014

The adjustment on the thyroid Meds continues to cause many roller coaster days of anxiety and depression. I understand it can take a year or even longer if you are a woman of my age. I'm only a few months into this.

I'm also mourning the change in a number of important friendships all at the same time from moves and other changes of circumstance.

Broken body, broken heart … It feels so overwhelming. But I'm trying to remind myself that The Lord gives and the Lord takes away … whether it be physical, mental, emotional, relational they are all gifts from Him and will neither come nor go except as His loving heart has chosen.

This is a good day to feel for the everlasting arms and try to find rest in them. Everlasting is one of the sweetest words of comfort I can think of today!

July 13, 2014

People are still praying and I'm still fighting but I had a much better day yesterday. Really enjoyed the sermon I heard on Ruth and God providing for us in remarkable ways. I'm always amazed at how God has done just that for me. This was exactly the sermon I needed but no one knew I would be there today to hear it but God! How He is always providing for His children!

July 15, 2014

Fears of what may be ahead are rising as the first results of blood work with cancer markers approach (appointment on July 31, the last day of Marks sabbatical!)

Thoughts run all over the place like untamed horses. There are various scenarios to consider of what the future will hold based on what these results show. But I know the truth is that these 'ponies' can be trained, tamed and contained by God. They can be taught to prance rather than buck. But it will take quite a strong bit or a really tall fence to do it.

So I'm putting on my jodhpurs and my boots with spurs and going to try to 'ride this little pony to town.' Hopefully by God's Holy Spirit inside me, God's Word beside me and my friends around me praying, I will get there.

I'm asking for prayer that I will rest the future with God and not spoil the last few weeks of this potentially restful time with Mark!

July 31, 2014

It's 5:30 a.m. and I'm feeling my 'clay' today. In five hours I will get my first results about my cancer from markers in my blood. I can see a fork in the road but can't quite make out which way the arrow is pointing. My future is so tied to what is or is not silently going on in my body – my 'clay'.

Grateful for Philippians 3:20 'but our citizenship is in heaven and we eagerly await a Savior from there'. Citizenship defines you. No matter where you roam or live, you have a passport that tells where you are from and there are privileges that come with that.

If you get in trouble, it's the embassy where you flee to. And in this passage it's who is there who will come and rescue you. 'We eagerly await a Savior' from there.

No one is like this Savior. He sends His Spirit ahead into our hearts to both calm us and embolden us. He sends His people ahead to encourage us and give us the warmth of love, affection and caring hands. He sends His Word ahead to remind us of what our homeland is like and what He is like. Our citizenship of the heavenly country comes with unshakeable promises for life here.

Yes! I eagerly await a Savior from there today! But through His emissaries – His Spirit, His Word, and His people – I am (so far) calm and confident that God is directing my path. He will save me from merely feeling the feebleness of my clay. Maybe, just maybe my crumbling clay will reflect a bit of Himself – the wonderful, powerful, permanent, triumphant Savior.

I'm grateful to be enjoying the lavish deep peace that only comes from God. Citizenship has its benefits, especially when traveling with friends like mine who care and pray!

From God's Word:
PSALM 18:27-29.

July 31, 2014
I won't get results of the cancer marker until tomorrow but the blood work was good and none of the lymph nodes are enlarged. Cautiously optimistic. If it's good tomorrow then my next appointment is in November and then a sonogram leading up to the radioactive iodine scan in January I guess.

August 2, 2014
Received the last of my blood work and my cancer marker is still there but decreased in half since March. It can

continue to reduce as a result of the radiation for another eight months so they are pretty happy with the direction things are going. It will be a long road but at least the sun is shining on this part of it! Grateful!

August 3, 2014
What a very different book the Bible would be if God always gave His people what they could handle. All my favorite stories that so clearly display His greatness would be gone. Praying that God would display His greatness in my life rather than simply provide the safest exit strategy.

August 5, 2014
I was listening to *The Lion the Witch and the Wardrobe* as I drove yesterday. I got to the part where Aslan comes back to life and tells Susan and Lucy that there is much to be done so they must get on his back. They have only his mane to hold onto as he leaps and bounds great distances … and even flies at one point … and they are thrilled!

I feel like Lucy and Susan being asked to get on board the lion (Aslan) and ride the life God has given me. It's scary for the feet to not touch ground – to not control where you go, how fast you get there, to not be able to balance yourself, and to see how great the heights from which you could fall.

It is not unreasonable to replace my fear of what's ahead with excitement. There is an adventure after all – the adventure of who God is! That would be incredibly wonderful! Got a long way to go in this but because of Him I will get there. I'm practicing holding on as He leaps today. ☺

August 12, 2014

> God is our refuge and strength, a very
> present help in trouble. 2. Therefore we will
> not fear … 4. There is a river whose streams
> make glad the city of God. 5. God is in the
> midst of her; she shall not be moved; God
> will help her when morning dawns. 10.
> Be still, and know that I am God. I will be
> exalted among the nations, I will be exalted
> in the earth! PSALM 46: 1-10

I never really understood 'the river that makes glad' part of this psalm until today. If you go and read all of this psalm you can see that it is an 'under siege' psalm. Someone is under attack and surrounded. Enemies stand guard around the walls of the city and force the people inside to stay inside. This means the enemy has blocked the way to the water outside the city gates. Without water the citizens will not survive … Or so the enemy hopes.

But look! There is a river IN this city! The people inside can survive! They can be glad!

God is this kind of refuge for us. We might be stripped of the 'watering holes' we usually enjoy if we are going through a season of trial. But this is meant as a painful kindness to us. Sometimes we get way too dependent on other things – and not God. Perhaps He's making it all the clearer to us that He provides the river that makes glad our lives. He takes other things away to draw us closer to Him. He takes them away to help us to be still and know that He is God, not the other things we enjoy or thought we needed.

And it makes no sense to others. Perhaps this is one way He exalts Himself before the nations. Showing that He does the impossible inside those who seek Him and trust in Him. He makes them glad.

August 14, 2014
I am thinking about how God holds together and sustains all things. That means every day and in every circumstance I am meant to be dependent upon Him.

I find that in my hardest times I hold onto God to bring me through but I'm also holding my breath, waiting for them to pass and I can relax again.

Relax into what? My self-reliance again! There are days when I know and live in His dependence and others when I ignore my need to rely upon Him. I guess that means my hard days are really my best days in some ways. They are God's insistent reminders that I must start with Him and finish and live in between.

August 14, 2014
What a wonderful occasion this is! I'm busting out of the stall big-time and driving to Louisville Kentucky to see my dear son and daughter-in-law. I'm going through the mountains of West Virginia and taking in all the green majestic beauty. Praying and thanking God for all that He has done, all that He is enabling me to do and the encouragement He's giving me because He will complete this work He's begun in me. Great is His faithfulness! Higher than the mountains around me deeper than the valleys and wider the skies above.

August 22, 2014

> For a little while you may have suffered grief in all
> kinds of trials. These have come that your faith may
> be proved genuine … . faith which is of greater worth
> than gold which perishes though refined by fire and
> may result in praise, glory and honor when Jesus
> Christ is revealed. 1 Peter 1:7

I am trying to learn what must be called contentment for
the day. Not waiting for this trial or that trial to be over,
but instead realize that they are the hunger pangs that God
wants to satisfy with Himself.

I treat these trials as my enemies, and one day they will
be all gone and that will be good. However, God intends to
use these trials as my friends. He brings them and tailor-
makes them for my good and His glory. So I'm going to
stop acting like I don't hear them knocking on my door. I'm
going to welcome them into my day and into my heart and
try to learn from them and through them.

From God's Word:
Isaiah 63:9

August 22, 2014

> Christians should pray that God will increase
> their faith so that they can appreciate His
> care and planning everything that happens to
> them. They should remember that they simply
> cannot understand all that God is doing with
> them. For all they know, God has a purpose to
> fulfill in their lives in twenty years' time which
> depends on something that is happening this

week. If they resist His will for this week, they
are resisting His will for all the other things that
depend on this week.

JEREMIAH BURROUGHS Learning to be happy

August 22, 2014

Why is it that my version of 'waiting on The Lord' looks
far less like delight and far more like tapping my foot
impatiently for God to hurry up and finish my to-do list?

August 24 – quote

Trust in God grows only as we become more and more
acquainted with Him – with His power, His goodness,
and His love. Trust blooms in the heart that has come to
believe that God in His love always wills what is best for
us. In His wisdom, He always knows what is best, and in
His sovereignty He has the power to bring it about.

ELYSE FITZPATRICK
Overcoming Fear, Worry and Anxiety

August 24, 2014

Interesting … If you think about the I Am's of Jesus, they all
presume a neediness.

I am the light of the world … Speaking to people who
feel the darkness.

I am the vine … Speaking to people who feel their lack of
self-sufficiency

I am the bread of life … Speaking to people who are
hungry and dissatisfied with what this world holds.

I am the resurrection and the life … Speaking to those who
feel their own deadness and the passing nature of this world.

I am the good shepherd ... Speaking to those who are lost and aware of their need of the protection and guidance of another.

This is good news indeed!!!

No wonder it's those who hunger and thirst for righteousness who will be filled. You have to be empty to be filled. It is a kind Father who empties the hearts and lives of His children to fill them with Himself.

August 25, 2014

I am editing three stories today that focus on God's faithfulness. The first one is about God's faithfulness and the unfaithfulness of the Israelites as they head towards the Promised Land. They have been freed from slavery in Egypt and they have heard the very voice of God. They have received God's good laws, and known His daily sustaining in the wilderness. Yet still when the spies come back from Canaan and they hear of the enemies they will have to face, they fear so much that they want to go back to slavery!

Oh! I don't want to be like them. I So want to be like Caleb and Joshua, the only two men that trusted that God was faithful and could and would do everything necessary to take the land.

I am as forgetful as the Israelites. Please Lord! Please help me to be changed because of how I have seen you work! Help me have eyes of faith and dare to rely on you to do great things! You are worthy!!! So worthy!!!

August 26, 2014

Just had the honor of seeing God answer a friend's month of prayers for a seemingly impossible situation in an absolutely amazing way. What seemed like a month of 'no's' from God burst into the most stunning 'yes'. Like a firework display of His power.

I realize that sometimes I feel like all my prayers for long-standing situations are just going to God's spam folder, never to be seen or answered … Just deleted.

But actually they are being stored up as just the right answers to be revealed at just the right time.

This makes me turn to prayer more fervently for situations and people I had begun to give up on. I realize more than ever that no prayer is forgotten or unanswered. No prayer is left unopened or unattended. No prayer is turned away powerless. Surely they grow in strength as they pile up and will all be delivered to us with just the right response in just the right time. And perhaps the longer we wait, the more amazing they become.

August 27, 2014

It has been a very reflective day today!

REFLECTION 1:

How easy it is to spend our days thinking about what comes next. This leads to worry about the bad things, impatience for the good stuff, and often employing distraction to help the time between today and that next thing go faster.

If we spend each day longing for the future to bring the next good thing or bring an end to the current hard thing, then when do we ever live today? So busy wishing it away for tomorrow!

What a waste of appreciation of the gift and beauty of the day at hand! This is the day The Lord has made. Let us rejoice and be glad in it! PSALM 118:24

REFLECTION 2:

I would love to live every day of my life like I was watching a suspenseful movie the second time through. I'd be aware that it was going to be an action-packed story, but could be completely confident that every risky, death-defying, twist and turn would come out with the hero on top and triumphant in the end!

God's promises to His children are that good. If anyone should be able to confidently savor life with all its unknowns and difficulties, it should be them!

Now to try to somehow build these reflections into my life!

August 28, 2014

Oh, what a safe place it is to be a follower of Christ in this dangerous world of ours!

From what I understand, joy and happiness are two very different things. Happiness is like a child's toy boat set to sail on the ocean, ready to be swamped by little more than a guppy-sized wave of difficulty. Joy is like a buoy, anchored by a long, strong chain to the rock bed of God and His Word, deep below. It bounces up and down on the top of every wave, yet even in a hurricane it holds firm.

I feel like I'm living just outside the borders of joy as a way of life. I can see that world of joy better than ever and want to live there. It excites me to know it is real and a possibility, but I'm not quite there. Like the sailor from the crow's nest who hollers 'Land Ho!' at the first glimpse of distant shore. The good news is I think God is the one moving me along in this direction. Chances are real good that I'm going to get there.

Afflicted saint, to Christ draw near –
Your Savior's gracious promise hear,
His faithful Word declares indeed,
That as your days your strength shall be.

REFRAIN:
So sing for joy, Dear afflicted one,
The balttle's fierce, But the victory's won,
He shall supply all that you need,
Yes, as your days, your strength He'll be.

Let not your heart despond and say
'How shall I stand the trying day?'
He has engaged by firm decree,
That as your days your strength shall be.

REFRAIN:

Your faith is weak, your foes are strong,
And if the conflict should be long,
The Lord will make the tempter flee,
For as your days your strength shall be.

REFRAIN:

Should persecution rage and flame,
Still trust in your Redeemer's Name;
In fiery trials you shall see,
That as your days your strength shall be.

REFRAIN:

When called to bear your weighty cross,
Or sore affliction, pain, or loss,
Or deep distress or poverty,
Still as your days your strength shall be.

REFRAIN:

So sing for joy, Dear afflicted one,
The balttle's fierce, But the victory's won,
He shall supply all that you need,
Yes, as your days, your strength He'll be.

JOHN FAWCETT 1740-1817
(Refrain by Connie Dever)

August 28, 2014

Contentment means letting go of knowing exactly what will happen to you and when it will happen, but holding onto God and His good purposes for you through it all.

It means letting go of knowing when and how help will come, but holding onto the fact that God will surely send it in just the right way and just the right time.

It means letting go and actually being joyful that God is writing His story with your life instead of what you come up with on your own.

Words of Wisdom:
Why am I so curious to know the reason of my Lord's providences and the motives of His actions? Will I ever be able to clasp the sun in my fist and hold the universe in my palm? Yet, these are as a drop in the bucket compared with the Lord my God. Let me not strive to

understand the infinite, but rather spend my strength in love. What I cannot gain by intellect, I can possess by affection. Let that satisfy me ... The least love to God and the simplest act of obedience to Him are better than the most profound knowledge. My Lord, I will leave the infinite to you and pray that you would keep me from a love of the tree of the knowledge that would deprive me of the tree of life. C. H. SPURGEON *Evening September 5*

'Trust Me!' the Lord says to His people every day. From the Garden to the Grave He always has done and always will do all things well.

September 7, 2014
Many times Endurance for us is moment by moment little trusts in God, all tacked together. The God who gives us everything we need for this moment will give us everything we need for all the other moments in our lives until He has completed every good work He has prepared for us and takes us home.

Jesus had joy as He endured the cross ... every bitter moment of it. It is amazing to look at such great joy and such great endurance as He went across that great gulf of suffering.

I certainly have no sight or strength of soul to look across so great a suffering and have joy. But perhaps if I focus on joy for the day or hour or even moment, these little joys will string together like pearls on a very long chain and will still shine with God's grace and glory from here to eternity.

September 8, 2014
At least some crucial element of self-control mustn't come directly from us, but from the Spirit of God within you!

Why else would it be called a fruit of the Spirit? That is of great comfort to me when I wrestle with changing a habit of thoughts or feelings or actions. He can do what I cannot!

But I need to take on board that part of Galatians 5 that talks about not gratifying the 'flesh'. That's my natural bent. That's where I need the Spirit's fruit of self-control.

September 15, 2014

Have you ever watched a stadium crowd hold up sheets of paper that together reveal a huge image that would be impossible to guess were you to look at just one of the individual squares? It is so fun to watch what is revealed.

I was thinking how each day of our lives is like one of those squares that we hold up. No two squares look alike in texture or color. There may be some elements that make sense as we look at it, but a lot that look like blotches. It doesn't make sense and won't until the whole picture is in place and is revealed, as we look at it from a distance.

Whether the piece we are given to hold up for this particular day has a few bits that we can make sense of or whether it is mostly blotch, we can boldly hold it up in its assigned seat, knowing that one day we will wonder at the perfection of its placement and its purpose.

But I must say, that the darker and more mysterious the blotches on my day's square, the greater the humility and faith I have to ask God for. I love to be my own life's interpreter and I love to know what it means today. All too quick to call into question the Artist behind it all who rendered the picture than curb my faulty vision and impatient, harsh interpretation of the little square He gives me to hold up today.

So I'm defiantly saying no to my Internal Judge today and turning to praise God for His compassion, patience and steadfast love which understands and forbears yet urges me to choose humility and ask for more faith. Who continues to do good to me, His child, even when I'm squirming in His embrace.

September 16, 2014
What a difference there is between someone who knows where their next meal is coming from and someone who doesn't!

The person who knows where the food comes from, comes to the table with confidence and with the question: 'what's for dinner?'

The person who doesn't know where their food will come from, comes to the table with dread and with the question: 'will there be any dinner?'

I would say that I'm someone who has had a relatively easy life and has lately had much bigger and more frequent struggles that are requiring far greater intervention and answers from God. I'm feeling like someone who went from knowing where my next meal is coming from to someone who isn't so sure. With this has come the change from confidence to panic about how various situations will work out that I cannot see an apparent solution to.

At least at FIRST I thought I was moving from confidence to panic. Now I'm beginning to think that perhaps I'm moving from an attitude of taking things for granted or even apathy (from a life of ease) to panic. I'm thinking that God is giving me true hunger to lead me to see that all along He has been and will be the provider. And to slowly but surely take me to confidence that He is always where the next 'meal' comes from and is dependable no matter how empty the cupboard looks.

Only God can take what feels like two steps backwards and turn it into a giant step forward!

September 18, 2014

Have you ever tried to compare one, single grain of sand to a whole expanse of a beach? Amazing to think that the span of our life will not add up to even as much as that piece of sand when compared with the stretch of eternity.

And yet, what happens within it is of such great importance that it affects, irrevocably, what happens within that whole, vast, timeless expanse.

So … what are we to do with this day?

> This is the day that The Lord has made. Let us
> REJOICE and BE GLAD in it. Psalm 118:24

This verse has been on my mind lately in answer to this question. Rejoice and be glad because The Lord has made the day tells me so much.

The Lord made the day. He has plans and is in control of it. He is faithful to His character and therefore I can trust that what He has planned for this day will be in keeping with His character. He is good, so I can rejoice!

The Lord made this day. He chose for it to be. His plans for this world would not be complete without it. It is filled with good works He has prepared in advance to be done by us as a part of it. Good works, though perhaps small, even for me! He gives me purpose and will give me ability. I can rejoice in that!

This is the day The Lord has made. There are no surprises or mysteries to Him, regardless of how confusing things may look to me. One day it will all be clear and He will have made it all beautiful in His time. I can rejoice in that!

Let us rejoice and be glad in it. There is a willfulness involved here, too. A setting of our eyes to a proper vision for the day and seeking a proper tone to our hearts. To cultivate a satisfied contentment, resting and rejoicing in the day because His 'everlasting arms' hold all of it up. A freed, peaceful busyness that comes from knowing there will be good fruitfulness that results from it, no matter how barren or menial what we do may seem sometimes. A mindfulness and expectancy that looks for, savors and expresses gratitude for God's goodnesses, aid and presence throughout it.

This is the day The Lord has made! Let us rejoice and be glad in it!

September 19, 2014

God kindly brought Joseph's life to mind this morning. How many times he thought he could see the end of his difficulties, only for one to be replaced by yet another.

Just think …

Boo … he's thrown in pit to die, but Yay! they pull him out.

Then, boo, they sell him into slavery. But yay Potiphar buys him and eventually puts him in charge of his whole household.

Then boo, he gets thrown in jail for years on a false charge of womanizing. But yay, an important official he helps promises to help him get freed.

Then boo, the official forgets, but biggest yay he finally remembers and Joseph becomes the prime minister and is in a position to rescue all of his family and continue the line of Israel that many years later brings the Messiah Jesus.

I don't know what Joseph thought through all those twists and turns. God had given him those big dreams early on. Perhaps God used them to keep on having faith as he thought relief was coming, but more difficulties came instead.

But for us, we have wonderful promises that 'All things work for the good for those who love God and are called according to His purpose.' And, to make all things beautiful in His time. And even to do more than we can think or imagine for our good and His glory.

So today, I'm asking God for relief … absolutely … as I face three, long-standing trials right now.

But I'm trying to turn up the volume on His voice as He is undoubtedly saying not just 'As your days, your strength shall be.'

But also 'Trust Me! Wait for it! You are going to thank Me for all this!'

If He was up to so much macro good through so much micro bad in Joseph's life, why will my life be any different?

September 19, 2014
It's amazing how many times in the Bible we are told to wait patiently for The Lord! Must be we regularly have a messed up sense of perfect timing.

September 20, 2014

Trying to understand the significance of something remarkable that happened today. It was one of those stormy days in which I felt overwhelmed with a handful longstanding of unknowns. I was at wits' end a number of times as the circumstances hit me afresh. I prayed, meditated in truths about God, exercised, soaked up Vit D in the sun, tried to turn my worries into positive thoughts, as well as do what I could to just make myself quit thinking about the things that are overwhelming me. Nothing really worked.

But then I shared what I was going through with a few people and asked them to pray for me. Within only a few minutes (at most), I felt the black cloud lift and peace replace the turmoil. And it's still gone!!!

Wow! Now I think all those things I tried were good things, but I think next time I won't wait to fight all day before I ask others to pray. I feel like I've called in so many 'prayer favors' this past year with what feels like day after day of weakness. It's hard to ask yet again. But it sure seems He is making a point: share with one another! Pray for one another!

September 20, 2014

Having learned my lesson last night, I'm asking you to pray for me today. At noon I have a child ministry workshop to lead that lasts about four hours usually. Pastors are here for the weekender event at our church as well as children's ministry people who specifically travel here for a workshop. Not feeling that great at all but have a few hours to rest before it starts. Please pray for clear thinking, stamina, wisdom and a number of grumpies in my body to settle down so I can lead this meeting well. Thank you!!!

September 22, 2014
Found a new way to (sort of) curb my fears and to see God's kindness in overwhelming situations. I began to thank God for what I am NOT facing right now. I'm so good at thinking up unhappy endings that I figure I might as well harness that skill for the good. And sure enough, I'm pretty good about thinking of things I would like to be going through even LESS than what I'm going through now. And looking at these things works to actually help me appreciate the trials God has given me and the loving limits He has placed on them. It's a bit backwards way to get to gratitude but I'm not complaining!

September 22, 2014
Dissecting what I'm having trouble relying upon God about into little pieces and asking Him to help me with each little part rather than as one big lump prayer as I usually do. Helpful to see the different threads and where I am so needy.

Kinda sad but perhaps appropriate that I am even having to ask God to rely upon Him to help me rely on Him. I think He surely must do that too. If not then I'm toast.

September 24, 2014
If there is one thing I'm convinced of, it is that God loves to show Himself able in impossible looking situations. Life after life of people in the Bible includes circumstances like these that God then did remarkable things.

With our God, a helpless feeling about a hopeless situation need be only that. A feeling! But it is a feeling that need not lead us to despair, but to prayer. It seems that the only thing impossible about an impossible situation is the impossibility for God NOT to act in behalf of His people and according to His character. Let's storm the throne of grace today for God to act and overturn even the most unlikely circumstances and untouched hearts!!!

September 24, 2014
Jesus being our Saviour, of course makes us think foremost of what He did on the cross to save us from the eternal punishment rightly owed us for our sins against our holy God. But looking at the lives of Old Testament and New Testament believers, you see them cry out for daily salvation. What a comfort that we have a Savior for eternity as well as all the little increments of eternity called days! Just think about what it means that we need and have a Savior! We are in over our heads in trouble, but it's not over His head. We may look and feel and actually be helpless, from the earthly standpoint. But that's what people who need a savior look like! We are right on track! And we have someone far better than Superman or Spiderman coming to get us!!!

October 1, 2014

> … in your book were written, every one of them, the days that were formed for me, when as yet there was none of them. PSALM 139:16

> He leads me in paths of righteousness for his name's sake … Surely goodness and mercy shall follow me all

the days of my life, and I shall dwell in the house of
the Lord forever. PSALM 23:3, 6

What wonderful meditations these promises make to those
who trust in Him! He planned out every day of our lives
ahead of time.

And what did He weave into each one of them?

His leadership showing us the way and making the way
for us to live His way (paths of righteousness). And His
goodness and mercy springing up along the way and getting
in line behind us. How long will be the parade of memories
of His goodness and mercy, if all the days of our lives they
are promised!

Today is a great day to appreciate the path God has
made for us! To look back at all the little (and big) goodnesses and mercies lumbering along the trail behind. To
look down and be grateful that we don't walk blindly and
aimlessly but have been given a special, tailor-made trail
that is perfect for us. To look side to side and appreciate
the 'scenery' of today's path that will be left behind in a
short twenty-four hours. And to look forward in faith
with as much gratitude for what's ahead as for what's been
in the past. We are on our way to the house of the Lord to
dwell forever.

And our shepherd promises to go ahead of us every step
of the way. There may be rocks and brush and fallen trees.
There may even be a few hungry bears along the way. But
our shepherd blazes the trail. He has removed the obstacles
that are too much for us out of the way and provided us
with all the footing and protection we need. How good is
the shepherd who leads us!

October 5, 2014

> Count it all joy, my brothers, when you meet trials of
> various kinds ... JAMES 1:2

Oh, how I am tired of trials! Oh, how I still dread what is coming next! As I approach the year mark of the tests that led to my cancer diagnosis, I'm fighting huge battles with uncertainty and fear. What will the next results show? When will I know that I'm safe? Will I ever enjoy that happy, restful, easiness that I knew before all of this began? There feels like there is nothing but shifting sand.

Yet this verse reminds me again. We can take joy in our trials because our God is purely good! There maybe much mystery but there is no malice in the trials He allows! There may be much uncertainty about what comes next, but none about His intent. And so, JOY can be ours! Actually, joy IS ours, even before the anxiousness settles down and while the tears are still wet on our face.

I am so quickly delighted by the wonderful things of this good world. But too easily, my delight turns into dependence upon them. Fears rise as it looks like they will be whisked away from me. The desire for a happy, care-free life becomes like a gilded cage. Good health, good times, good family and friends are precious gifts for us to enjoy, but seeking our happiness in them makes a merciless master in a fallen world like ours.

For me, it seems that trials come in like time release reminders of how real God is, how great He is, how much He loves us and how much better both He and the world to come are.

And so ... The whole section, not just verse two ...

> 2. Count it all joy, my brothers, when you meet trials
> of various kinds, 3. for you know that the testing
> of your faith produces steadfastness. 4. And let
> steadfastness have its full effect, that you may be
> perfect and complete, lacking in nothing.

How can I really desire something less than COMPLETE?!! This is what He is up to! This is His wonderful design!

Oh, to GRATEFULLY, take up the joy that God offers to me today and to thank Him for the trials that He has sent to serve me far more faithfully than all my favorite people and things!

October 9, 2014

Each day I have a choice to inform my faith through God's Word and through remembrances of His work in the past. I have a choice to choose His expertise as best.

And each day I have a choice to trust, to secure myself into Him. Faith – informed and secured.

Both take mindful effort, at least for me. Constantly I'm having to call myself away from living in the house built upon the sandy, unsturdy soil of my own understanding and going back over to the construction site in the hard, rocky soil of my heart where the house of God's making is going up very slowly.

Yet, the more I build here, the more prepared I am for whatever comes.

When the storms of difficulty come, my own understanding has proved to be incredibly weak to withstand their fury.

But what has my kind Heavenly Father done in times like these? Used them to beckon me back to the house on the rock!

But how much better to set up my construction site there each day in the first place!

Spurgeon Quote

> Wherefore hast thou afflicted thy servant?
>
> NUMBERS 11:11

Our heavenly Father sends us frequent troubles to try our faith. If our faith be worth anything, it will stand the test. Gilt is afraid of fire, but gold is not: the paste gem dreads to be touched by the diamond, but the true jewel fears no test. It is a poor faith which can only trust God when friends are true, the body full of health, and the business profitable; but that is true faith which holds by the Lord's faithfulness when friends are gone, when the body is sick, when spirits are depressed, and the light of our Father's countenance is hidden. A faith which can say, in the direst trouble, 'Though he slay me, yet will I trust in him,' is heaven-born faith. The Lord afflicts His servants to glorify Himself, for He is greatly glorified in the graces of His people, which are His own handiwork. When 'tribulation worketh patience; and patience, experience; and experience, hope,' the Lord is honoured by these growing virtues. We should never know the music of the harp if the strings were left untouched; nor enjoy the juice of the grape if it were not trodden in the winepress; nor discover the sweet perfume of cinnamon if it were not pressed and beaten; nor feel the warmth of fire if the coals were not utterly consumed. The wisdom and power of the great Workman are discovered by the trials through which His vessels of mercy are permitted to pass. Present afflictions tend also to heighten future joy. There must be shades in the picture to bring out the beauty of the lights. Could we be so supremely blessed in heaven, if we had not known the curse of sin and the sorrow of earth? Will not peace be sweeter after conflict, and rest more welcome after toil? Will not the recollection of past sufferings enhance the bliss of the glorified? There are many other comfortable answers to the question with which we opened our brief meditation, let us muse upon it all day long.

Morning and Evening (October 7th)
by C.H. Spurgeon

October 9, 2014

So grateful for those who have gone before me and this pilgrimage of life with God. Grateful that they have been willing to share their perspective from the higher altitudes of what they see of the goodness and beauty of God.

I may be lower down in the valley, but their writings call down to me and describe things from above that I can't see yet in these lowlands. Beautiful, Amazing, exciting things! Encourages me to look for the next foothold that will take me up just a bit higher today. Especially grateful to Mr and Mrs Spurgeon! How the Lord has used that couple in the lives of millions, even on a daily basis! If you have not read any of Mrs Spurgeon's writings, then you have a real treat in store for you. Lord has used her every bit as much as He has used her husband in my life.

. I waited
ne and
e pit of
set my feet
He put a
se to our
their trust

morning! Wait ....
ice! Yay for the pro-
ouragement that it is

I'm still fighting so
; conquered by now,
ies of needed patience
and times of waiting are as sure as the promise of deliverance!

I guess we would like our hearts to be ready and finished as fast as a chicken tender gets cooked on a hot grill. But the truth is, our hearts are as hard as shoe leather and it will take the long, slow simmering of a crockpot of many days and even years to turn them into what they should be. So yes, it's OK that it takes a long time. He is at work even if it is just a tiny bit each day.

October 17, 2014
There's something very tiring but very freeing about realizing that you may have to fight some battle in your heart every day.

Instead of wishing for my heart to just behave and not react fearfully or sinfully in another way and dreading the 'damage control' of confessing sin, finding God's truth and applying (over and over) to whatever the particular issue is, I'm beginning to accept that something will come each day and that's OK.

There's my grocery list, my oh-my-what-a-mess-my-house-is to-do list, my email/phone list, my work to-do list, and now there's my heart battle to-do list. And it's pretty clear that the heart battle to-do list is the most important of the lists by far.

October 17, 2014

> Cast your cares on the Lord and he will sustain you.
> He will never let the righteous fall. PSALM 55:22

Was thinking about how going through life with God is a bit like two people with very different strengths and abilities going on a multi-day hike together – a strong leader and a little wimpy follower. Together, the two will need to take all that is needed in terms of food, clothing, bedding, maps, etc. But if they divide the supplies in equal shares and each carry what each needed, then it would be way too much for the little wimpy guy to carry. He would be overburdened. And so, they divide up the supplies in terms of what each can carry.

I suppose this puts the little weakling in a very dependent position. After all, the other guy is carrying many of the essentials for the trip. If they get separated, what will he do? By casting his burden on the other guy, he is placing his very life upon him.

God is like the strong, very capable leader and we are like the little wimpy follower. There are many things in our lives that we try to carry but they are simply too much for us. We like to hold them ourselves because it seems safer to hold them in our hands, but we just aren't cut out to carry them and make the journey. So God calls us to cast our burdens upon Him and have Him carry them. And with them, our lives.

It is hard to hand over so many basics of life to Him, but traveling lighter, carrying only what He calls us to is such a relief when we do it. And with His promise to never leave or forsake us, we know that we and all we entrust to Him is safe.

> When you walk through the waters, I will be
> with you; and through the rivers, they shall not
> overwhelm you; when you walk through the fire
> you shall not be burned, and the flame shall not
> consume you. ISAIAH 43:2.

October 22, 2014

Many times when a loved one is going through something difficult, I wish I could change it and change it now! I love them and I hate to see them suffer.

But the trouble is when my heart races along to panic because I can't change them or the situation, and it leaves me. … and them … in what feels like a hostage situation. My hands are tied, therefore the situation is hopeless.

And then the Lord brings the comforting truth to the mind of me, His silly sheep who is obviously suffering delusions of grandeur.

Only He is needed. He often may make me useful to fulfill His good plans. Perhaps I will get to bring a word of hope, a hand of help, a persistent prayer that He has chosen to use in the fulfillment of His plans but only He is needed.

What a world of difference between being useful and needed! The control side of me likes to grab the wheel or speed up the clock, but really there is something wonderful about knowing God only calls us to be useful rather than needed. He can prevail! He will prevail!

October 23, 2014
I've decided that one of the bravest women in the Bible is the widow who put in all she had to live on into the Temple offering. I think of all the women in the Bible I would most like to be like her. She would have had little or no regular means of support. Yet her total trust in God to provide for all her needs was what gave her both the ability and desire to offer everything up to God. Wow! What a woman! I am so NOT like her! But, as Richard Sibbes writes in *Bruised Reed*, a seedling is called a tree, even if it is very small. It does not look like a tree, but we call it one because that is what it will become.

And, I'm coming to believe that perhaps it's only with time and weather and storms that little seedlings become strong trees. Perhaps it was not until that woman lost her husband, that God taught her that kind of trust. I would much rather 'read the book' or 'watch the movie' than learn by experience when it comes to this. But, it's becoming quite clear to me that that is not typically how God works ... or perhaps the point is that it's not really how we work. So onward and upward by God's grace.

October 24, 2014

> Submit yourselves therefore to God. Resist the devil,
> and he will flee from you. JAMES 4:7

One of the best things I can remember each day is that this life is a fight for things greater than a striking number of good and easy days strung together. And, that since God has an enemy, so do those who love God. This enemy loves to tempt us with his lies and stir up mutiny in our hearts so that we distrust and rebel against our good God and His amazing plans. We are in for a fight!

When I remember these things, it helps me see the lies of the enemy for what they are and resist them. It helps me remember what he is like and what God is like. Why would I possibly take the lying whispers of this cruel enemy over the promises of my good God? I've got to fight back!

If you ever read *The Silver Chair* by C. S. Lewis, you might remember how the witch of the underworld tries to enchant the children and Puddleglum with her lies, telling them that there was no Narnia, no world up above. If she can do this, then she can defeat them. Puddleglum sees himself giving into her lies and thrusts his hand into the fire to shock him into remembering the truth. He does remember, defies the witch and helps all the others do so, too. The witch's spell is broken.

I'm certainly not suggesting burning our hands is a good idea, but I do admire Puddleglum for doing what he needed to do to wake himself up to the lies that were trying to settle in his heart. This was the enemy speaking! He would not believe! I love that! A marsh wiggle (what Puddleglum was) must be the homeliest creature of Lewis' making, but his courageous defiance was beautiful. Definitely adding him to my hall of heroes I would like to be like!

October 25, 2014

Jesus said I love you to us and to God His Father with three words ... NOT MY WILL. He said these as He asked God His Father to let Him be spared the cup of suffering and dying on the cross for the sins of God's people. Then Jesus said ... but not my will, but yours be done.

Amazing! All of His life, Jesus taught He had come down from heaven not to do His own will, but the will of Him who sent Him – God the Father. Yet this was such a terrible, terrible thing He was to endure! He did not want to suffer like this!

What love Jesus has for us and for God His Father! God, help our response be like Jesus'. Help us to grasp the depths of your worthiness for any sacrifice we might go through as part of your plan. Fill us with your Spirit and help us to love like Jesus.

October 26, 2014

> I will remember the deeds of the LORD; yes, I will remember your wonders of old. Psalm 77:11

Memory is selective. What we remember seems to be a combination of our brain's ability to hold information as well as choose what to recall.

Part of this is just plain ole brain chemistry. Some of us can store more information and are better at storing certain types of information.

But a second part of memory is also a determination of significance. We help shape what we remember by what we spend time thinking about as it happens and as we choose to recall later because it ranks in significance for one reason or another.

Yet a third part of memory seems to be interpretation of the meaning of what we have experienced, or learned. We can even forget incidents but still store up judgments we make based on them – Judgments that affect how we think, act and react to other situations.

Wow! What a powerful opportunity we have to use what we learn or what we go through each day to strengthen truth or lies in our head! No wonder it is so important to read and memorize God's Word as well as calibrate our senses towards looking for God at work in each day.

What will I feed my memory with today? What will be stored up in my mind's yearbook and seep into the reservoir of my heart?

God, help me be deliberate to recall your wonderful works, to place full value upon them, and to etch an unforgettable, true picture of you in my mind and heart. Grateful we can ask your Holy Spirit to work inside us to help us to see you and remember you: how good and faithful you are.

Open the eyes of my heart, Lord! Record your deeds and your true character indelibly upon my mind! Let me see you and your mighty acts around me and enjoy a growing confidence in your steadfast love and faithfulness!

October 28, 2014

> Now to him who is able to do immeasurably more
> than all we ask or imagine, according to his power
> that is at work within us. EPHESIANS 3:20

The 'bad' news about God being able to do exceedingly more than I can imagine is that I will not be able to lean upon my own understanding as He is doing the wonderful things that only He can do. There will be many times when it looks like He is NOT doing more than we asked for or imagined….or as much as we asked for or imagined … Or even anything at all like what we asked for or imagined.

But that shouldn't put us off! What do we expect if God is going to work in such huge ways?! God and His plans for His people are so purely good that instead of being discouraged when they veer so far from what we thought, we can dare by faith to thank Him in advance for what amazing things He has planned. And that is the very very good news!

October 29, 2014
When I was a pre-schooler, I can remember activity times when the teacher would distribute little mounds of play dough to each of us to play with. Everyone had their own bit to create their own masterpiece and no one was to mess with anyone else's creation. Most kids were pretty good at respecting each other's personal dough space. But some-times the boys would reach over and stick their fingers in their neighbor's work. It was just too tempting.

The memory of this came to me this morning as I was praying. I noticed how many of my prayers are like sticking my hands in God's playdough rather than tending to my own little lump. What do I mean? Well … I'm so busy poking at His timing, His plans, the outcomes of things, His wisdom, etc. instead of being happy to let Him be the potter and do what He wants with the clay of life. If anything, I need to be asking Him to be sticking His fingers more into my clay and working what He knows is best in me.

Please, Lord, help me to delight in your will and pray that it be done. Help me not to be praying in a way that is really wanting you to change your good will. Help me to pray for whatever you want to do. Help me to welcome you to poke at my heart and life, shaping it into whatever you want it to be. Make my prayers filled with requests for trust, confidence, delight, expectation, surrender to You. Fill me with the knowledge of You and your love that exceeds anything that I can comprehend.

October 31, 2014

Blessed be the name of God forever and ever, to whom belong wisdom and might.

21. He changes times and seasons … he gives wisdom to the wise and knowledge to those who have understanding;

22. he reveals deep and hidden things; he knows what is in the darkness, and the light dwells with him.

23. To you, O God … I give thanks and praise, for you have given me wisdom and might,

and have now made known to me what we asked of you, for you have made known to us the king's matter.

This was part of Daniel's response-prayer as The Lord rescued he and his friends from certain death.

They along with the other Magis had faced death if they could not tell the king his dream and its meaning.

The king had refused to disclose the dream to them. They were Magi. They were supposed to be close to the gods. The gods should tell them the dream and its meaning if they were the real deal, the king told them. When the other Magis could not give the king what he wanted, he put them all in jail, sentencing them to death.

So the king's officers came knocking on Daniel's door telling him that he and his buddies would be joining the rest of the Magi in prison. They too would be killed.

But Daniel and his three friends countered. They asked for time to pray to The Lord and ask Him for what the king wanted.

The Lord answered their prayers and revealed both the dream and its meaning to Daniel. Daniel praised God with the prayer that's written above.

I love that our God knows all things! Even the deep and hidden things that lie in darkness!

My life today and as I look forward to the future is full of things that I classify as deep and hidden. How encouraging it is to realize that everything lies open to our God! And not only does He SEE all, but He is the one who plans all and works in all...and always for His glory and the good of His people.

If I lack wisdom He promises to give me all that I need. And the things that He withholds from me, it's because He's holding them for me, Himself, in His hand. It's mind-boggling to start to tally up all the things God takes care of for me! It's one of the wonderful things about reflecting back over situations and seeing how God was at work in them that I can only see now.

If God's faithfulness reaches to the skies, each of our lives are like sparkling rainbows, glistening with color as the light of His perfect work shines out upon our past tears and leaves a beautiful display of His goodness from start to finish.

He will feed His little sheep – all His little sheep – what they need and will take care of the rest Himself. How good He is! Oh to dare to trust Him, with a heart full of confidence in Him and appreciation of His long-suffering, perfect care! Oh, to dare to have child-like faith! Oh, to boast in The Lord with my life! I hope to have a feast of looking back today upon His faithfulness in my life rather than worry about what lies in darkness ahead!

Today is Halloween and everyone is dressing up as something! I intend to try to go as a child today! And will try to keep wearing this costume on my heart every other day!

November 3, 2014

> 17. For this light momentary affliction is preparing for us an eternal weight of glory beyond all comparison, 18. as we look not to the things that are seen but to the things that are unseen. For the things that are seen are transient, but the things that are unseen are eternal. 2 CORINTHIANS 4:17-18

What if the very trials we dread will happen in the future or try to get out of today are the very things that God somehow will make the currency of our joy in heaven? What if the very things we would love to cast away now wind up being the benefactors of our greatest gifts in heaven? Something like this must be true if they are preparing for us an eternal weight of glory!

If so, then not only can we rest in God taking care of us as we go through hardship and thank Him for however He might use these trials for our good and His glory here. But, be excited that it is like we are a blindfolded child wrapping his own present, being guided by the hands of a loving Father. We know the present is before us, but we can't see exactly what it is. He puts the tape, the paper, the ribbon, even the scissors in our hands and guides our movements with our hands in His. We hear the rustle of the paper, snip of the scissors and feel the shape of the gift. But it won't be until opening day in heaven when the blindfold is taken off and we see what wonderful gift it was that God was giving to us and even used us to wrap.

November 4, 2014

> For the moment, all discipline seems painful
> rather than pleasant, but later it yields the peaceful
> fruit of righteousness by those who have been
> trained by it. HEBREWS 12:11

Painful now ... Pleasant ... peaceful ... Righteousness later. LATER hmm.

How much later? Sometimes it feels like an eternity!

Oh, Lord, help me to be trained by your discipline! Bring later now!

November 7, 2014

Magnificent promises NOT from Revelation, but hundreds of years earlier in Isaiah.

Lord, you are my God;
I will exalt you and praise your name,
for in perfect faithfulness
you have done wonderful things,
things planned long ago ...

He will swallow up death forever.
The Sovereign Lord will wipe away the tears
from all faces;
he will remove his people's disgrace
from all the earth.
The Lord has spoken.
In that day they will say,

'Surely this is our God;
we trusted in him, and he saved us.
This is the Lord, we trusted in him;
let us rejoice and be glad in his salvation.'

ISAIAH 25:1,8,9

From start to finish, God is the same! From start to finish, His plans will succeed! Let us rejoice in this!

November 8, 2014

OK ... So there's just no other way to put it, but I am having a terrible struggle with sadness and fear right now! Was up hours last night in the throes of it.

Wednesday is the ultrasound of my neck and it will be the first deep look for cancer since the radiation treatment in March. Then next (in a month or so?) will come a little radiation to look for it throughout my body. This is normal procedure at the one year point, but there isn't anything that feels normal about it. That's the thing with cancer, I guess, you are always waiting for it to come back. It's one of those circumstances in life that is a yoke you wish you could throw off, but you have to learn how to wear it by God's grace instead.

I feel like I'm being battered in a storm of turmoil inside with this. The only difference from now and last year is that now I am able to more readily praise God for His goodness and I feel more confident that He will be helping me through.

It's like I'm a spectator as well as the one going through this. The one going through it is terrified perhaps as much as ever.

The spectator part of me recognizes that my emotions and fears are different from the firm reality that God is with me and will help me no matter what. He is the rock. He is the refuge where I can flee to tremble within. Don't like trembling at all, but better by far to be terrified with His huge, merciful arms wrapped around me and under me than standing out in the storm all alone.

> The Lord Himself will fight for you, you need only
> to be still. Exodus 14:44

November 9, 2014
Loving the book: *The Hardest Peace* by Kara Tippetts. Expecting grace in the midst of life is hard. The author is a young woman with four kids going through stage four cancer, but for anyone going through 'hard' as she calls it.

Here's a quote she includes in her book:

But because I believe God's plans for me are better than what I could plan for myself, rather than run away from the path He has set before me, I want to run toward it. I don't want to try to change God's mind – His thoughts are perfect. I want to think His thoughts. I don't want to change God's timing – His timing is perfect. I want the grace to accept His timing. I don't want to change God's plan – His plan is perfect. I want to embrace His plan and see how He is glorified through it. I want to submit.

NANCY GUTHRIE, *Holding on to Hope*

Here's another quote from Kara, herself:

Receiving what is before me and fighting to walk in the path that is only lit one step at a time is a daily practice. There are days the truth comes quickly and days the struggle to hear beyond the lies of comfort, security and health feels impossible … . I still have a long journey of seeking grace that I may never understand, but this journey has taught me so much. Perhaps the humbling, the prying open up my hand to time, and the growing imaginings for my forever tomorrow's has become the balm to help me see truth in the midst of pain. The lessons have come, but they haven't come easily.

Cancer is a gift. It is the gift you never wanted, the gift wrapped in confusion and brokenness and heartbreak. It's the gift that strips all your other ideas of living from you completely. The beautiful, and the ugly raising to the surface of the importance of each and every moment.

KARA TIPPETTS

FYI: *Holding onto Hope* by Nancy Gutherie (quoted above) looks like another really good book on suffering especially if you're someone who has dealt with the loss of a stillborn child.

November 9, 2014
OK one more quote from Kara Tippetts book. Wow!

> (A quote from *The Hardest Peace*) Whoever listens to me will dwell secure and be at ease, without dread of disaster. PROVERBS 1:33

> When we listen – really listen – to the Lord, looking Him straight in the face, He removes the dread. It does not say He removes the disaster. But the dread of disaster. If I really sit and listen to God, He will lift the dread. The dread and fear are what so often steal our peace and leave us on the edges of our moments exhausted.

> We meet the scary of life and forget to turn to God and listen and know His peace. We scramble to control, fix, and protect from hard. The imagined fears and worries often break us more than the reality ...

> With that, I can also take note that sometimes when the dread enters, I'm not doing the hard work of quieting my heart to listen. This is a constant struggle. I'm too often ready with words instead of the needed quiet. The entering of dread is a new litmus test of my healing.

> Trust me, moments of dread come. They steal joy, create chaos and fear, and leave me utterly wrung out. Dread exposes my fear and weak faith and failure to trust or my eternal security rest ... .

> I bowed my head and asked Jesus if He would help me take hold of this new, startling truth. I prayed to live present in the gifts and callings of today without

dread of tomorrow. I asked and I expected, and trusted that in knowing and listening, I would find peace and comfort.

The whole book is this good. One of the things I love about it is that she's writing from the middle of her struggle, not at the triumphant end when trouble has passed. She's seeking a triumphant middle in each and every moment of each and every day.

I'm a lover of happy endings. When I'm particularly low, I will sometimes put on an old favorite movie to watch the happy ending. Don't misunderstand me here ... I fast forward it to ONLY watch the happy ending! I so want to see everything work out! But Kara's book encourages me to put the happy ending in each moment, cherishing the gifts of it and the opportunity to fill it with joy now in God's wisdom and plans and loving hand...not waiting for the happy ending that will come.

November 10, 2014

It's 4 a.m. and I've been fighting the fear monster in my heart all night. I keep waking up to such fear. Am grateful for Kara Tippetts' book because she describes the fight of dread so well and what to do. .... Stare at the eternal God and who He is. Stare at His goodness. Rest there. Praise Him for the good plan that somehow includes all of this. Kara is right. It does help. It is work. And I'm tired.

I feel like getting my heart to rest where it should be is like pushing a huge stone up a hill into place for it only to roll back down again. I have to get up and push it back up the hill again and again and again. Oh, for it to stay put! I'm so weary! I know with muscles, repeated effort leads eventually to greater endurance and strength. God's Word says the same is true of our heart ... but right now I am just feeling the burn and the fatigue.

If this is a couch to 5k of my heart, I feel like I've not made much progress. But at least I don't think I'm still sitting on the couch with the popcorn and the remote in my hand. God has definitely got me up and moving... Just not very far along in my training I guess.

The thing is ... I have no particular reason to think that they may find anything on this test. It may very well be all clear. It's just the unknown of it and the remembrance of last year as well. I have fifty-four hours until the test and who knows how much more until they call me with results. I don't want to worry my way through these days, but oh it is so hard!

I guess I need to think of it as being tempted to worry but fighting back. Then it's still really hard but not a waste. Perhaps it's really good then. I WANT to want what God knows is best, even if it's a path that includes more cancer. I certainly can see how He's using it to work in me and bring me closer to Him ... I just don't want it.

Thanks for praying!

November 10, 2014

> I remain confident of this: I will see the
> goodness of the LORD in the land of the
> living. PSALM 27:13

I think I understand this passage better than ever. How encouraging! It's not a promise that everything will change to rainbow shiny bright happy here but that God promises to give us eyes to see His goodness in whatever it is we face. He can do this because He is the one that makes all things work for the good of those who love God and are called according to His purpose. (Rom. 8)

He sets the bounds on our life struggles and plans the fruit that will come from the sorrows sown. That is why He can give us this promise to see His goodness … Because He has made sure that it is there, woven into it all.

I am so grateful to be found in Christ! I am so grateful that while I still squirm under the thought of suffering and eventually death, that Christ swallowed up the punishment, the sting of death for me! That cup He wanted to pass from Him the night before He died on the cross included all that I would have had to drink myself and I would have been feeling the terrible suffering from it eternally. But now … By His huge free gift, my body will one day be put in the ground, but as a seed. It will spring up to life.

The suffering I face here is numbered … Perhaps the number will be equal to my days here, but it will NOT go beyond them!

Now to see this, most surely, is to begin to see God's goodness in this land of the living – or dying, as I guess it really is. And oh how much more of His goodness I will see in the land of the eternally living!

November 11, 2014
Thank you all so very, very much for praying! It was an amazing answer to prayer day! The Lord took away my anxiety all day and it still is gone! So appreciate you all

fighting on my behalf! Going to try to sleep tonight! Here goes!

November 14, 2014
Just wanted to thank you for praying and tell you that I got the all clear this afternoon on my ultrasound! Very grateful for all your prayers! And for the results!

November 21, 2014
Everything God created reflects His character in some way or other. Usually it's the mountains or a beautiful sunset that gets my attention as they declare God's beauty and majesty.

But today it's something completely invisible that He made that is reminding me about Him. It's gravity. How like His promises to never leave us or forsake us!

We can't get away from gravity. Every step we take, everything we do, we have to take it into consideration. What a wonderful picture of God's faithfulness to us! How like the everlasting arms that are underneath us always.

November 29, 2014

> But he [the Lord] said to me, 'My grace is sufficient for you, for my power is made perfect in weakness.' Therefore I will boast all the more gladly of my weaknesses, so that the power of Christ may rest upon me. For the sake of Christ, then, I am content with weaknesses, insults, hardships, persecutions, and calamities. For when I am weak, then I am strong. 2 CORINTHIANS 12:9-10

Paul's contentment and boasting rests on one little phrase...
'for the sake of Christ.' Just like Jesus, his contentment
rested in knowing that what he faced would not primarily
FEEL good but would BE good – for God's glory. That is
what they both desired most of all.

Content with ... weaknesses, insults, hardships, perse-
cutions, calamities. Those words encompass all the troubles
we go through or dream up.

Content for only one reason....for the sake of Christ.
Paul wanted his whole life to be used up to show how
great God is. So while he hates the suffering, he accepts
the opportunity as something better. He is no sadist. He
doesn't enjoy pain, yet he remembers his wonderful Savior
and what He did to save him. He remembers that this life
is an endurance race with a glorious prize at the end for
those who press on. So having just asked God three times
to remove a terrible source of suffering, he now cries, 'Bring
on any of those things that by nature, men dread.'

So, like Paul, I take a deep breath, swallow hard, and ask
God to make my life a stage for boasting in Him for any
around me to see. My obvious weakness an the opportunity
to show His obvious strength.

November 30, 2014

> Now there is in store for me the crown
> of righteousness, which the Lord, the
> righteous Judge, will award to me on
> that day. 2 TIMOTHY 4:8

What's missing in this picture? My righteousness! No
way will I or any of us deserve a note-of-mention, let

alone a CROWN when it comes to righteousness. Sin, foolishness, stubborn willfulness…now maybe we might be in the running for the prize for that, on the day we stand before the Lord, the righteous Judge. Nope! A righteous Judge who judges me on my own works would have only one terrible, very deserved verdict for me. Eternal punishment!

Yet, not this righteous Judge! He will give me a crown of righteousness, because He gave me His perfect righteousness for my very own. He took my punishment, Himself so He could do this!

Nothing like thinking about that Day and that reward which I will receive, because Christ has given me HIS perfect righteousness to make me more grateful and more desirous to praise Him and cheerfully do whatever He would ask of me!

Tis the season to be jolly … but even more, tis the season to be joyful, grateful, boastful in and because of the Son that God gave us to save us!

Immanuel arrived … at just the right time. MATTHEW 1:21-23

December 1, 2014
I don't know if old dogs can learn new tricks but they certainly can teach them!

Our sweet old dog is having a lot of difficulty with our bare wood stairs. This is a big deal because there are FOUR flights of stairs to get up to our bedroom where she insists on dragging her hurting self up to sleep with 'the alpha female of the pack' (me) every night. She slipped down a few stairs and every morning we faced her fear of going down them.

At first, we tried to keep her from coming up, but she was so miserable all alone downstairs that we let her come up anyway. A number of times we just picked her up and carried her down, but she is NOT a small dog and I was afraid we might lose more than a dog if this kept going.

So, I devised a 'magic carpet' approach. I lay a towel down and hold it in place for her to walk down. She stops at the end of the towel, and waits for me to lay a second towel down before she walks down the next set of stairs, etc until she's down them all.

At first Esme (our dog's name) was terrified as she waited for me to lay down the next towel, but after a couple weeks of this, she now is, if anything, over confident of my ability to quickly get the next towel in place. She runs down those stairs and it's everything I can do to get the next towel in place in time. She is that confident that I will take care of her.

Having had a hard wee hours of the morning that spun out into worry about some things later today, God provided me with this wonderful picture. Every day, I may have to face my set of 'slippery' stairs of fears and circumstances, but like Esme – and really far, far more – I can run forward towards the day, having full confidence that God will provide whatever I need just in time to help me get through them.

So you see, my old dog certainly taught me a new trick.

PS … I have been told of stair tread carpet pieces that I can purchase, so I think my magic carpet trick can be retired soon. ☺

December 4, 2014

What a day of feeling my total inability to change myself! What a miserable fight it has been today! Yet, how kind of the Lord to provide me with friends to listen and pray … and Himself to forgive.

Here is a wonderful quote from a wonderful book called *Extravagant Grace* that I was reading tonight as I try to make sense of it all:

> John Newton observed that God seldom frees us from besetting sin before showing us how deeply inability is rooted in our souls. If this work were cooperative, with me and Jesus working together, then at the end of the performance there would be two people on stage taking the bow. However, understanding my inability leads me to a far different posture. I am not on stage next to Jesus, taking a bow. Instead, I am flat on my face in the dust, with my hand on my foolish mouth, worshiping at the feet of my beautiful Savior whose power and grace has rescued me.

This book springboards off of John Newton's thoughts that God has allowed sin to indwell in His people to show them the depths of His love and grow their relationship with Him as they learn their utter dependence upon Him. Very, very good.

> Do not be anxious about anything, but in everything, by prayer and petition, with thanksgiving, present your requests to God. And the peace of God, which transcends all understanding, will guard your hearts and your minds in Christ Jesus. PHILIPPIANS 4:6

December 6, 2014

> May the God of hope fill you with all joy and peace
> in believing, so that by the power of the Holy Spirit
> you may abound in hope. ROMANS 15:13

Hope is forward-thinking that rests on God's ability to do all His good plans in this world through us, without us and even in spite of us.

It is a new pair of shoes for worriers to put on to walk through life. We like to look at the road ahead, but hope can use this tendency to have joy, peace, even excitement and anticipation of what God will do with what is ahead. And to pray.

Worry is what we do when we look forward godlessly. Hope is what we have when we look forward god-centeredly.

> Worry is not believing God will get it right, and
> bitterness is believing God got it wrong. TIM KELLER

December 8, 2014

Thank you for praying!!!!! How God helps me when you pray!

Cancer numbers still going right way pretty much. I have one number that needs to go to zero that isn't there yet. Looks like another small dose of radioactive iodine next April to take another look to make sure about the cancer. If that's good, then maybe won't ever have to have another one of those.

The hardest thing was she confirmed that my current psychological state of trigger happy, physiologically induced anxiety is my new normal. ☹

So ... It's only over to the psychiatrist to see if there is something I can take that will help me not be so miserable.

I'm sad as I process this info but God is good and means good through this. He will be my daily shepherd.

Thanks for praying!

December 12, 2014

I wonder how many of the things that God allows in His people's lives that don't make sense right now are because He is running ahead of us, providing what we need before we even know we need it.

In heaven, there will be nothing but looking back. It will all make sense and we will see that God indeed does all things well and there is no darkness in Him or His ways at all. It will be clear vision.

Faith is looking around, looking back, and looking ahead now, realizing that we do not have the vision to see all that God sees yet. It is acknowledging ourselves to be short-sighted, if not outright blind. It is to (fight to) rest in His leading us through, depending upon His perfect sight. His Word is like our Braille. It helps us to know that which we cannot see.

December 13, 2014

New favorite part of Scripture. Mary and Martha's words to Jesus when He's going to Lazarus tomb 'but Lord he's been dead more than three days ... he stinks! Or as another version puts it. ... There will be a stench!'

Can you imagine! So dead that you are decomposing and you stink. Yet even that is not too much for the Lord to do something about it! Why should I not have hope for anything He wants to do in me today? Why should you not have hope for anything He wants to do in you today?

Even more amazing is if you think about the fact that the Lord deliberately stayed back so that Lazarus would die and would be dead for four days and so that there would be stinking. Then He would bring him to life! God planned this. This would be a stench for His glory!

December 16, 2014

On great faith days, we can look farthest forward into the days of our lives, feeling confident of God's faithfulness for them all.

But some days are small faith days, as difficult circumstances weigh us down and we wonder how long they will last and how will we ever keep going. Looking forward at times like these can be a huge temptation to be overwhelmed if not terrified. At least for me.

But I guess on small faith days like this, we can lower our gaze to looking down to our feet…where we are this very moment. God is faithful right here, right now. My eyes can see that, though maybe just that. And we can work to put a roadblock up for our thoughts, dwelling right here or on His past faithfulnesses.

He will take us through every other small slice of the future this same way, if need be, until it is all finished and we are with Him in heaven. Surely He is just as faithful to those whose eyes are cast down, monitoring their halting baby steps as to those who can look out confidently and go forward in giant strides.

December 27, 2014

Thinking about godly ambition this morning …

Godly ambition is doing everything we do to the glory of God. Yes …. Check … That's the way I usually think of it. But I'm realizing how there's still so much of my own lovely agenda and perspective that gets to thrive there. I like this kind of godly ambition. I try to live here every day.

But on this side of heaven, there's at least one more kind of godly ambition. And this kind has a way of convulsing the not-so-godly ambition that is happily lurking in our hearts when we think we are doing everything we LIKE to do to God's glory.

It's the kind of godly ambition that accepts the fork in the road that takes you off the path you loved and thought you would always enjoy, and over to another one that your heart does not leap to take.

This kind of godly ambition acts by humbly asking God to fill that path with all He desires. With His definition of success. And to fill your heart with as much satisfaction with His plans (that weren't yours) being accomplished as you had when His plans (which were yours) were being accomplished.

My heart is convulsing a bit these days along such a new path. And as it convulses, I detect frustration, irritability, pity and a number of other lovely responses.

How kind God is to shepherd me to where He knows is best, even though I'm grumbling and do not want it.

And how so unlike Jesus, the most amazing picture of godly ambition. Who said 'no' when offered the kingdoms of the world the easy way, in order to be the sacrifice to bring us to God. He came knowing He would suffer. Both a path He did not look forward to and would rather not take, yet a path He would never veer from. He was faithful, perfect, ambitious for God's plan to the very end.

What a life! What a Savior! Lord, make me a bit more like You today! You saw the whole path with all its sorrows and you delighted to do Your Father's will. Help me as I see just a little bit of the path, with its little share of sorrows, to delight to do My Father's will in it today.

Now faith is confidence in what we hope for and assurance about what we do not see. Hebrews 11:1 Faith is confidence. Confident in God's ability. Confident in His wisdom. Confident in His goodness. Confident is a wonderful word. It can be so helpful when our feelings are haywire or we are trying to figure how something will come about.

Yes, confidence in God is so wonderful because it requires neither of these things. No perfectly lined up feelings. No plan A or B of 'how' that I cook up is even needed. It's simply 'God can do and will do what His perfect plans have ordained.'

There's a such a child-likeness about this confidence in God. So many of the details are left to the One who knows and cares. It's like the very upset young child who stops crying before whatever their trouble is fixed, as soon as they see their parent. They are sure he/she will fix it, even if the how isn't known.

Unto us a Son is given ... . and with Him all things. We can rest. We can hope. We can rejoice!

DIARY
●●●●● **2015** ●●●●●

January 2, 2015

Leaving 2014 behind, but hopefully not a lesson from the Christmas season. Thinking about the two ways that Christmas is celebrated: as a DAY or as a SEASON.

The day of Christmas is a day of opening. Mysteries revealed ... often in quick succession, with the sound of much ripping paper, especially if you are a child.

But the season of Christmas is called Advent – or Coming. It is a time of reflecting on the parade of promises God gave us from the beginning of time of the coming Savior with 'healing in his wings' as one writer put it.

All those promises were like little tears in the wrapping paper that took centuries to at last completely reveal the gift that was prepared for us. Little tears, little revealings. Lots of waiting, lots of persevering, lots of hope for this great Coming.

I realize how much I like to live life like a Christmas Day. Lots of revealing, little waiting, all in quick succession. Ah, but God seems to call us to live our lives like Advent instead. Waiting, hoping, little tears in the paper for what all His big promises will do in our lives.

I guess my resolution for 2015 would be to try to live an Advent life. To spend each day content while waiting, gratefully expectant of God's daily provision, humbly not requiring to see the whole 'why' of the events of my life at once, but savoring the goodness and hope He shows me as He reveals a bit more of the gift of His wonderful story in my life in the 'little tears in the paper' each day brings.

January 3, 2015

Been thinking a lot about the Lord's Prayer lately. ... Give us this day our daily bread ... Reminds me of the Israelites in the wilderness and the manna The Lord gave them.

The Lord put them in that situation so that they would have to ask Him each day for what they needed. They accused Him of taking them out to the wilderness to abandon them and let them die. He was doing it to teach them that 'man does not live by bread alone but on every word that comes from the mouth of a God.'

Their thoughts: cut off earthly supply to harm them.

His thoughts: cut off the earthly supply to bless them with something greater – dependence upon Him and content-ment in His faithfulness in the midst of their helplessness.

Asking God to give us our daily bread is really not just asking God to supply us what we need but to also asking Him help us to be content with only getting our daily bread ... when many times we really want to own the bread factory and make certain of a lifetime supply of our own making.

January 5, 2015

One year ago today I had my thyroid surgery! Been a good day to reflect on the goodness of God in placing me on a road I would have never chosen, knowing He would use it to do things in my life that I really needed.

And thank you for supporting me through much of this year!

January 6, 2015

Wonderful, encouraging words from an old classic: *Knowing God* by Packer:

> What matters supremely is not the fact that I know God, but the fact that He knows me.

> I am graven on the palms of His hands. I am never out of His mind. All my knowledge of Him depends on His sustained initiative in knowing me. I know him, because He first knew me, and continues to know me.

> He knows me as a friend, one who loves me; and there is no moment when His eye is off me, or His attention distracted from me, and no moment, therefore when His care falters.

> This is momentous knowledge. There is unspeakable comfort – the sort of comfort that energizes – in

knowing that God is constantly taking knowledge of me in love, and watching over me for my good.

There is tremendous relief in knowing that His love to me is utterly realistic, based at every point on prior knowledge of the worst about me, so that no discovery now can disillusion Him about me, in a way that I am so often disillusioned about myself, and quench His determination to bless me.

There is, certainly, great cause for humility in the thought that He sees all the twisted things about me that my fellow – men do not see and that He sees more corruption in me than that which I see in myself.

There is, however, equally great incentive to worship and love God in the thought that, for some unfathomable reason, He wants me as His friend, and desires to be my friend, and has given His Son to die for me in order to realize this purpose.

We cannot work these thoughts out here, but merely to mention them is enough to show how much it means to know, not merely that we know God, but that He knows us.

January 7, 2015

Your affliction does not jostle your prosperity; it promotes it. Your losses do not cause loss; they increase your true riches. Press on, for you are loaded with untold blessings. Every event is marching for the righteous and the humble spirit. God will have His way in the whirlwind. Be patient, and wait on Him with childlike confidence.

The day will come when you will be astonished that there was a order in your life when you thought it all confusion. You will be astonished that there was love and you thought it was unkindness, there was gentleness and you thought it severity, that there was wisdom when you were wicked enough to impugn God's rightness.

Believer, the events of history march as a victorious legion under a skillful leader. Do not think we can order our affairs in better style. Our good, ill, joy, and grief keep their place. They do not push one another; everyone marches in his own column. JOEL 2:8

> CHARLES SPURGEON –
> *Beside Still Waters: Words of Comfort for the Soul*

January 7, 2015

In posting that Spurgeon quote, I couldn't help but wonder how many people The Lord affects even daily through that man's words, spoken so long ago! Isn't it amazing the power God has placed in words! Like little puffs of wind that no one sees, our words can nonetheless chill or irritate, calm or invigorate deeply the souls of men! What a powerful tool He has given us! We are junior craftsmen who have opportunities to do good with our words, following in a small way after our Master, who brings things into being and works so much good with His powerful Word.

Oh, to use this gift of words to encourage others today!

January 10, 2015

Lately I'm running into the challenge that the truest, best, most God-glorifying way of life is that one in which involves a glad heart towards God and what He calls me to.

Ran into this yesterday in Spurgeon in the morning passage of *Mornings and Evenings* for January 9th.

Ran into it today in John Piper's little book, *The Dangerous Duty of Delight*, as he quotes multiple passages in the Bible as well as thought-provoking quotes from C. S. Lewis and Jonathan Edwards as well as some of his own.

The best known Piper summary of this is 'God is most glorified when I am most satisfied in Him.'

The bottom line is my affections matter. Yes, it's good to go on and serve, act, think, live in accordance with truth, whether we feel it or not. But we do not have to simply give up and live there.

God wants our hearts to be filled with contentment and joy. He wants the beat of a joyful heart to match the good works of our hands as we do what He calls us to do. And actually, according to all these various godly men, this is some of the most excellent fruit that any good work of ours can bear.

Hmmmm … I think I have a long way to go here.

Sometimes a glad affection towards God and serving Him comes easy, such as when it is something I like or I can see the benefit clearly. But sometimes it is not, such as when it is something I don't like or cannot see the benefit clearly. But is that really contentment and joy in Him? I have a feeling the answer is 'no' here.

John Piper says to do three things:

1. Confess your joylessness.

2. Pray for God to restore the joy of obedience.

3. Go ahead and do the outward duty of obedience in hopes that doing it will rekindle delight.

I'm sobered by how disconnected my obedience and my affections have become at times during the hard days that I've experienced lately. But I'm excited to think that God who created good works for me to do, most certainly has also included growing affections of joy, contentment and delight in Him to be part of them.

Surely He must delight to answer prayers for this!

> God is most satisfied with us when we are most glorified by him. JOHN PIPER, www.hopeingod.org
> – PHILIPPIANS 1:12-26, Sermon, October 13, 2012.

January 14, 2015

> 'Fear not Abraham, I am your shield; your reward shall be very great.' But Abram said, 'Oh Lord God, what will you give me, for I continue childless, and the heir of my house is Eliezer of Damascus?' GENESIS 15:1-2

Years earlier the Lord promised to make Abram into a great nation. And yet even still he was childless. It appeared that God's promises would never come true. Yet The Lord kept promising to Abram: 'I am your shield; your reward shall be very great.'

But time has a way of wearing us down. The promises that seemed big and exciting and right around the corner, begin to feel like fairy tales as we lose our expectation of their arrival. Hopelessness threatens and we begin to wonder if the good things God promised us will ever come, or if like in Abram's case, they will only come in a very different form than expected. (Oh goodie, you gave me Eliezer to be my heir, when what I really thought You planned to give me was a son.)

But Eliezer wasn't the answer to the promise. It was to come. Abram had to keep waiting, and eventually the promise was fulfilled… And keeps on being fulfilled through this day and to the end of this world. God not only gave Abraham Isaac as his son, but also through his descendents came Jesus. And through Jesus, God has given Abram many more sons and daughters of the promise, and has indeed been a blessing to the whole world.

What great encouragement it is to me as I see a few Eliezer's in place in my life and the lives of others around me. Things long prayed for, yet still not coming as I so hoped they would. Will it always just be Eliezer? Or one day will the real gift come to take Eliezer's place?

This passage is a great reminder that the Eliezers are but placeholders. God is always faithful to all His promises. One day they will each be replaced by the full, rich blessings He promises. And they will be more than we can imagine too.

January 16, 2015

> … I trust in your unfailing love; my heart rejoices in
> your salvation. I will sing to The Lord, for he has been
> good to me. PSALM 13:5-6

These sound like words of rejoicing and thanks at the end of a good day or at least at the end of some big trial. But the fact is they come in the middle of great unrest, pain and yearning to be free from a long-standing trial.

This psalm of David starts with these words: 'How long, oh Lord? Will you forget me forever? How long will you hide your face from me? How long must I wrestle with my thoughts and every day have sorrow in my heart? How long will my enemy triumph over me?' (vv. 1-2)

This is a psalm of juxtaposition. There is a little word 'but' that stands at the beginning of verse 5 that I left out of my first quote to make the contrast more apparent between the life of David's feet and the life of David's soul. BUT I trust in your unfailing love. (i.e. This sure doesn't feel best, but I know that you know best. My understanding defers to Your wisdom.)

What a wonderful, encouraging testimony! I am so grateful for David's honesty and fight that he shares with us! How great is our God that no trial is too big that He cannot fill us with faith to trust in His good, no, perfect ways in our lives.

And, If you want a good book (written for kids but filled with much adult-sized truth) that is a great encouragement of God working deliberately for good even in mysteriously hard circumstances and trusting that He is, read *The Back of the North Wind* by George MacDonald. I've been listening to it on librivox.org. A free public domain resource for many older books.

January 17, 2015

> Here is a trustworthy saying that deserves full acceptance: Christ Jesus came into the world to save sinners – of whom I am the worst. But for that very reason I was shown mercy so that in me, the worst of sinners, Christ Jesus might display his immense patience as an example for those who would believe in him and receive eternal life. 1 TIMOTHY 1:15-16

How wonderful it is that God uses the worse we have to make His greatest display of patience, forgiveness and grace! I don't know that Paul really was the worst of sinners. I think we all feel like we are sometimes. Not really sure how you score that anyway. But the point is that there is enough mercy and it is given freely and gladly.

Grace enough for my sin! For my doubts, my grumblings, my fears, my willfulness! What good news this is!

And, on top of that, when I testify about His sufficient forgiveness for my abundant sin, He turns my life into a welcome sign for the gospel to others.

January 17, 2015

> 17. And I pray that you, being rooted and established in love, 18. may have power, together with all the Lord's holy people, to grasp how wide and long and high and deep is the love of Christ. EPHESIANS 3:17-18 NIV

Just try to find the bottom of this love of God! Just try to swim to the far side of it. You would be far more likely to do this, than ever find the end of God's infinite love. Wider and deeper than the sea. Wider and higher than the heavens.

Imagine being stuck out in the middle of the ocean with no boat or even life preserver. No land is even in sight on the distant horizon. How hopeless to think that you would have to choose a direction and start swimming in hopes of eventually reaching land.

That is how hopeless it is for those who trust in Christ to get away from God's love. To be in a situation that is not within His grasp. To be abandoned by Him. The only thing hopeless about a hopeless situation is that we would have to go through it without God. It just cannot be.

HERE IS LOVE

Here is love, vast as the ocean,
Lovingkindness as the flood,
When the Prince of Life, our Ransom,
Shed for us His precious blood.
Who His love will not remember?
Who can cease to sing His praise?
He can never be forgotten,
Throughout Heav'n's eternal days.

On the mount of crucifixion,
Fountains opened deep and wide;
Through the floodgates of God's mercy
Flowed a vast and gracious tide.
Grace and love, like mighty rivers,
Poured incessant from above,
And Heav'n's peace and perfect justice
Kissed a guilty world in love.

Let me all Thy love accepting,
Love Thee, ever all my days;
Let me seek Thy kingdom only
And my life be to Thy praise;
Thou alone shalt be my glory,
Nothing in the world I see.
Thou hast cleansed and sanctified me,
Thou Thyself hast set me free.

In Thy truth Thou dost direct me
By Thy Spirit through Thy Word;
And Thy grace my need is meeting,

As I trust in Thee, my Lord.
Of Thy fullness Thou art pouring
Thy great love and power on me,
Without measure, full and boundless,
Drawing out my heart to Thee.

January 20, 2015

> Immediately the father of the child cried out and said,
> 'I believe; help my unbelief!' MARK 9:24

I am so grateful for the account of this man's struggle! I used to think that faith was an all or nothing thing. But I've come to find that faith, like so many other things that are gifts from God, have a timely element to them: He gives more when we need more.

There are many times when a new difficulty comes and I seem to have so little faith that it's almost like I'm blind to God being here at all. I wonder, 'if I'm responding like this, with so little confidence that God is at work or that God will act, perhaps I really have no faith at all?'

But I've learned to walk through truths again: 'Do I believe God is the creator and king of this world?' Yes.

'Do I believe that I have sinned against Him and deserve His just punishment?' Yes.

'Do I believe that Jesus died on the cross as the perfect payment for the sins of all who would ever turn from their sins and trust in Him? Do I believe He rose from the dead in victory?' Yes.

'Do I choose to turn away from doing things my own way and place myself in His hands, to His care and to live life for Him?' Yes I do.

And then I realize that I still do believe …These truths of the gospel and many more.

But perhaps I need to ask for faith to face the new difficulty that is before me today. Like the man in this story, I need God to help my unbelief.

I am so glad that God never gets tired of us asking Him for what we need! Because I don't know about you, but for me, it's another day in the wilderness. I see a lot that looks dry and forbidding. Setting up camp, looking for water and food, but the stream bed is dry and not a food source in sight. How am I going to survive???

But there's God. There is God. And what a God He is! May He rain down food from heaven! May He bring water from the rocks!

May He take this sissy, weak-kneed woman of only a little faith, and strengthen her for the day. May He give me faith to let go of sight. May He give me faith to accept that I am finite, so very finite, and do not need to try to fix everything or have every answer or see what's around the corner.

Oh, for enough faith for it to be OK to let God be God. And to relax into His infiniteness and be a child! Oh, how I want to be a child with the confidence that He has everything in hand! It is the truth I most want to know deeply in my soul. It's what I'm asking for today! And the good news is, I think this is the very kind of prayer God delights to answer.

January 21, 2015

From *Keep a Quiet Heart* by Elizabeth Elliot:

> The worst pains we experience are not those of the
> suffering itself but of our stubborn resistance to it,

our resolute insistence on our independence. To be 'crucified with Christ' means what Oswald Chambers calls 'breaking the husk' of that independence. 'Has that break come?' he asks. 'All the rest is pious fraud. And you and I know, in our heart of hearts, that that sword-thrust is the straight truth.'

'If we reject this cross, we will not find it in this world again. Here is the opportunity offered. Be patient. Wait on the Lord for whatever He appoints, wait quietly, wait trustingly. He holds every minute of every hour of every day of every week of every month of every year in His hands. Thank Him in advance for what the future holds, for He is already there. "Lord, you have assigned me my portion and my cup" Psalm 16:5. Shall we not gladly say, "I'll take it, Lord! Yes! I'll trust you for everything. Bless the Lord, O my soul!"'

You keep him in perfect peace whose mind is stayed on you, because he trusts in you. ISAIAH 26:3

January 23, 2015

I'm finding that one way to grow gratefulness and improved vision for God's trail of goodness in my life is to think 'what if this were my last day?'

All there would be is looking back. When I do this, sure enough, all I see is God's faithfulness to me. He has always provided. He has always acted kindly and mercifully, though has never left off the discipline I needed. He has given me sweet friends, an incredible husband, my dear children and their spouses, and most of all, Himself.

He has borne His fruit in my life and allowed me to be a part of His good works that have been far better than

I could ever deserve or dream of. The sweet things have been oh so sweet. The bitter pills always necessary and palatable (though sometimes just barely). Pressed down and overflowing. All the days of my life. His steadfast love has endured all through my little 'forever'.

What a difference it makes in my thoughts to turn around and walk up the path God has given me, back first! All of a sudden, the gratefulness flows!

Usually I would think walking backwards would make me more liable to stumble and trip. But in this case, I think it may be looking at the path ahead that makes me stumble and trip even more!

> Give thanks to the Lord for his steadfast love
> endures forever. PSALM 136

January 23, 2015

> Give thanks to the Lord with the lyre; make melody
> to him with the harp of ten strings! Sing to him a
> new song; play skillfully on the strings, with loud
> shout. PSALM 33:2-3

Okay, true confessions. If I have an obsession about anything it is musical instruments. I love music and I love learning new instruments. I've had a long list of instruments that I wanted to learn and had gotten through it all with the exception of one. A harp. On the one year anniversary of my cancer I went and got a harp. It has been so delightful to learn! Largely because even if you're really slow at it it sounds beautiful. Actually it's hard for a harp to not sound beautiful in just about anything you do. What a wonderful instrument! Very welcoming!

My harp is a folk harp, not like the huge ones you see in the orchestra. It stands about four feet tall and has thirty-four strings. But when I was at the harp store, they had harps in much smaller sizes. I think maybe the smallest one might've been one with sixteen strings. None of them were small as the ten string harp mentioned in this psalm.

Now if you're used to playing a piano or something like that, you're used to an instrument that has a lot of variety. I'm finding the thirty-four strings on my harp about as small as I would like to go. Much smaller and the possibilities of what I can play goes way down.

But that's why I think that this verse from Psalm 33 is so amazing! The encouragement is to play skillfully on the harp of just ten strings. Just ten! That's just two notes more than octave. Not a lot of wiggle room. And yet is it not a good picture of encouragement for our lives?

There may be many days when we feel we don't have more than ten strings worth to play upon.

Sickness, weakness, any number of limitations may make us feel like we haven't much to offer. And yet the encouragement is to play skillfully on what we have.

Surely if a ten-stringed harp was good enough for the magnificent temple of the Lord in Old Testament times, then my small ten-stringed heart is enough to make a new song that pleases the Lord today.

January 24, 2015
Why would we ever want to live life, with all of its difficulties, on our own! The twists, turns and mysteries of it are hard enough with God. I can't imagine living through it without Him!

I'm so grateful to be living in life's storms within the hedge of His protection, given to us through His Son and His promises. It makes it okay that we don't understand everything. It makes it okay, whatever we go through, because we know He is with us and He is at work in absolutely everything! What does not make sense to our pea-sized brains, perfectly makes sense to Him.

If you trust in Him, how rich you are! If you do not yet, come and find safety, love and assurances that match every day and every trial!

Psalm 34 reminds me of some of the wonderful assurances we have as His children:

1. I will bless the Lord at all times; His praise shall continually be in my mouth.

2. My soul makes its boast in the Lord; let the humble hear and be glad.

3. Oh, magnify the Lord with me, and let us exalt His name together!

4. I sought the Lord, and He answered me and delivered me from all my fears.

5. Those who look to Him are radiant, and their faces shall never be ashamed.

6. This poor man cried, and the Lord heard him and saved him out of all his troubles.

7. The angel of the Lord encamps around those who fear Him, and delivers them.

8. Oh, taste and see that the Lord is good! Blessed is the man who takes refuge in Him!

9. Oh, fear the Lord, you his saints, for those who fear Him have no lack!

10. The young lions suffer want and hunger; but those who seek the Lord lack no good thing.

11. Come, O children, listen to me; I will teach you the fear of the Lord.

12. What man is there who desires life and loves many days, that he may see good?

13. Keep your tongue from evil and your lips from speaking deceit.

14. Turn away from evil and do good; seek peace and pursue it.

15. The eyes of the Lord are toward the righteous and his ears toward their cry.

16. The face of the Lord is against those who do evil, to cut off the memory of them from the earth.

17. When the righteous cry for help, the Lord hears and delivers them out of all their troubles.

18. The Lord is near to the brokenhearted and saves the crushed in spirit.

19. Many are the afflictions of the righteous, but the Lord delivers him out of them all.

20. He keeps all his bones; not one of them is broken.

21. Affliction will slay the wicked, and those who hate the righteous will be condemned.

22. The Lord redeems the life of his servants; none of those who take refuge in Him will be condemned.

January 25, 2015
Two verses that are very interesting to put next to each other:

For what does it profit a man to gain the whole world and forfeit his soul? Mark 8:36

And Matthew 6:31-34:

> 31. Therefore do not be anxious, saying, 'What shall we eat?' or 'What shall we drink?' or 'What shall we wear?' 32. For the Gentiles seek after all these things and your heavenly Father knows that you need them all. 33. But seek first the kingdom of God and his righteousness, and all these things will be added to you.

I love that the very things of life, sweat and death here are merely add-ons for God's people, from God's perspective.

Oh, to not be distracted and to own all the reality of this promise! To work hard at doing and enjoying God and all the good works He has prepared in advance for us to do!

As surely as a loving parent makes sure to have good food on the table, day after day when their children come home from school, chores or play, God will always provide for His dear children's needs every single day.

They don't have to worry if there's money enough, food enough, time enough or concern enough. Their Father knows all that they need. It will be waiting there for them steaming hot and full of flavor, without them having to wonder at all!

Thank you, Heavenly Father!

January 27, 2015

Two remarkable verses with mind-blowing comfort!

> And he awoke and rebuked the wind and the raging waves, and they ceased, and there was a calm … And

they were afraid, and marveled, saying to one another,
'Who then is this, that he commands even wind and
water, and they obey him?' LUKE 8:25

Simon, Simon, Satan has asked to sift all of you as
wheat. But I have prayed for you, Simon, that your
faith may not fail. And when you have turned back,
strengthen your brothers. LUKE 22:31-32

Who then is this who loves us and bears us through each day,
along paths of righteousness for His name sake and to bless
us with a cup that overflows with blessing? (Ps. 23). None
other than He who is even powerful enough to command
the wind, water, all of nature. He who has stronger prayers
than our greatest enemy. The wind may blow around us. The
wind may blow in our souls. But Jesus is stronger than all of
the storms … Oh how He loves those who trust in Him!

January 28, 2015
Just stumbled upon this …

> The Everlasting Arms
> Are you sunk in depths of sorrow
> Where no arm can reach so low;
> There is One whose arms almighty
> Reach beyond thy deepest woe.
> God the Eternal is thy refuge,
> Let Him still thy wild alarms;
> Underneath thy deepest sorrow
> Are the everlasting arms.
>
> Other arms grow faint and weary,
> These can never faint nor fail;
> Others reach our mounts of blessing,

These our lowest, loneliest vale.
Oh, that all might know His friendship!
Oh, that all might see His charms!
Oh, that all might have beneath them
Jesus' everlasting arms.

Underneath us – oh, how easy!
We have not to mount on high,
But to sink into His fullness
And in trustful weakness lie;
And we find our humbling failures
Save us from the strength that harms;
We may fail, but underneath us
Are the everlasting arms.

Arms of Jesus, fold me closer
To Thy strong and loving breast,
Till my spirit on Thy bosom
Finds it's everlasting rest;
And when time's last sands are sinking,
Shield my heart from all alarms,
Softly whispering, 'Underneath thee
Are the everlasting arms.'

By A. B. SIMPSON

The eternal God is thy refuge, and underneath are
the everlasting arms … DEUTEROMY 33:27

I think I will ask God to help me write a melody for it. I would
love to have these words floating through my heart.

January 29, 2015

The Lord is the strength of his people; He is the
saving refuge of his anointed. Oh, save your people

and bless your heritage! Be their shepherd and carry
them forever. PSALM 28:8-9

I would guess that most shepherds prefer sheep to use
their own wobbly little legs to get from point A to point B.
Maybe on occasion a lamb or a hurt animal needs carrying.
How wonderful it is that we have a shepherd who we can
ask to carry us all ... And can carry us for forever, as David
says. The Lord is our strength. He is our transport. He is
our saving refuge. He carries us Himself, making sure we
are safe and all will make it home. This fits so well with that
poem that I posted last night on The Everlasting Arms!
What an amazing God we have!

January 30, 2015

> Let the morning bring me word of your unfailing love
> ... I remember the days of long ago I meditate on all
> your works and consider what your hands have done ...
> For I have put my trust in you. Show me the way that
> I should go for to you I entrust my life. PSALM 143:5, 8

The banner over the starting gate of each day's race of life
is 'Whatever may come, God will be with us, helping us.'
The banner over the finishing line as we put our head on
the pillow will always be, 'My grace was sufficient.' Is there
any day when you can say that was not true, believer? There
is not for me.

Therefore, whatever the conditions of turf under our feet
in today's race ... 'let us throw off everything that hinders
and the sin that so easily entangles. And let us run with
perseverance the race marked out for us.' (Heb. 12:1)

And do so with child-like faith and joy! Our God is good. He is in control and works out all things marvelously!

> I can only spread the sail; Thou! Thou! must breathe the auspicious gale. C. H. SPURGEON

January 30, 2015

I have officially bucked and fought and scratched at God all day! Ugh! Just don't like the way He is doing (or not doing) some things. I have been an ugly mess! Then tonight I cried out to Him to change my heart. There is no rest without Him!

He kindly encouraged me tonight in a book called *Craving Grace* by Ruthie Delik. Here's some bits of it that certainly spoke to me:

> In repentance and rest is your salvation; in quietness and trust is your strength, but you would have none of it. ISAIAH 30:15

> Repentance takes me to the root of my unbelief. It forces me to consider what I am trusting instead of Christ … I will battle my unbelief daily! So daily repentance means I need to recognize when I am listening to lies, confront the lies with the truth, and ask God to help me repent of the unbelief that led me to cling to the lie in the first place! …
>
> Repentance begins with conviction. The goal of conviction and confession is to soften my heart and open up the door of repentance. Paul David Tripp describes it like this, 'it's only when I am grieved by my sin and acknowledge that this sin is heart deep

that my confession will be followed by the turning of repentance'.

The tricky thing is that repentance really is a work of the Spirit. It's a gift He gives us that restores our relationship with Him and brings healing. It's not something we produce as a way to manage our sin or fix ourselves. It's an internal shift caused by the Holy Spirit that sets us on a different path. It is a change that will show itself not only in a transformed heart but in transformed attitudes, behaviors and relationships. Repentance is a work of the Spirit; it's a gift He gives us that restores our relationship with him.

Somewhere along the way, we discover that repentance is not possible without surrender, without the 'I quit.' Repentance is positioned to lead to restoration. But I know from experience that before you taste that restoration, it will feel like you are dying. It will smell like death. Because it is. Repentance is a dying to self, letting go of what you are clinging to, and admitting it isn't working. The uncurling of your fingers from trying to squeeze one more drop out of what you thought would bring you life is going to feel like it will undo you. But it won't.

The goal of repentance is to remind me who God is and how much He loves me and to take me to the cross and straight to His arms. And that is where the party begins! ... I am forgiven, and my relationship with God is restored. I am loved. That's why it says in Romans 2:4 that God's kindness leads us to repentance. It is such a sweet gift!

Oh how I need this repentance that leads to restoration and peace tonight! So glad that He works in us to bring us back to Him again and again! That is kindness, indeed!

January 31, 2015
Was thinking how the sin and sorrow of this world are like diseases that ravage in us and around us in this good world God made. In our hands, in our hearts and in our minds, they can be, and too often are powerful, destructive forces.

But God is like the scientist who creates a vaccine from these deadly diseases to heal the very ones sick and dying from it. He wields it with complete competence and control, and uses its very power to bring healing.

Our enemy likes to point out that God seems to be caught red-handed wielding disease, in hopes of getting us to turn on Him and accuse Him of wrong-doing. But the truth we must remind ourselves of is that God is the only one who knows how to use the brokenness and even sin of this world for good purpose. We want Him to be right there recycling it, harnessing it, getting rid of it. His fingerprints can be seen on these difficulties in our lives. But they are not indications of His malpractice. They are the marks of His unspeakable kindness and mercy.

He cares enough not to simply let us go on our merry way to destruction, but to send His Son to live here in our mucky world to bear our sins in His body. And if that wasn't great enough, He cares enough to promise us to be at work for good in every bit of our lives…down to the most broken, most diseased parts.

January 31, 2015

A little 'back story' behind at least my recent rumblings … Perhaps you will pray … Sounds stupid I guess … I have a routine colonoscopy scheduled for Monday and I'm terrified they are going to find cancer.

Not having any signs, it's just once they find cancer (my thyroid cancer was out of the blue) when you weren't expecting it, then that party is waiting to happen in your head so quickly again.

So … I'm fighting all sorts of fears and need to rest in God. With whether something will be found or not and what that would mean if they did. The thought of dealing with more cancer sounds so much more than I could bear right now.

I know … There probably won't be a trace of anything. But I'm rehearsing it all over and over in my head. Ugh! So please pray for my test and maybe even more, for rest in God instead of anxiousness.

February 1, 2015

Wanted to thank everyone for praying for my fun procedure but it turns out that I have to re-schedule. Oh well… . More fun to come I guess smile emoticon thanks again for praying.

February 2, 2015

> COUNT it all joy, my brothers, when you meet
> trials of various kinds, for you know that the
> Testing of your faith produces steadfastness. And
> let steadfastness have its full effect, that you may be
> perfect and complete, lacking in nothing. JAMES 1:2-4

COUNT it … Value it like this, even something 'feels' or at face value is a trial. An act of faith and will many times.

Count it ALL … . Nothing is wasted. Even the most hideous, heart-wrenching parts.

Count it all JOY …

Lasting, God-given delight because of these trials … down to the last drop.

Why?

So you will lack NOTHING.

He is testing our faith to make it stronger, so we will lack nothing. Apparently this word 'testing' in the Greek has a positive meaning of being an agent to bring about something good, not the negative one that may first come to mind of checking up on us and seeing how well we do.

All our trials, our testings, are for our good to do good … And so we can count it all good … we can count it all joy!

Life is a bit like childbirth labor and delivery – without the epidural! Ha!

We love the break between contractions because with them comes a break in the agony. But it's the painful contractions that do the work that brings new life. There would never be the birth if there were no contractions.

God seems to typically mature His people the same way. He gives them wonderful, sweet seasons of good things, but wisely sends us difficulties to do much of the good work of change He has in mind for us.

Amazing! The things we enjoy most here are only momentary tastes of the greater good things He brings us through these trials. God's ways are so different from ours, are they not?

We set out to be happy building sculptures in the sand, that are amusing with only a few hours' work, but destroyed by a passing wave. While He chisels deeply into marble fiber of our very deepest parts, leaving a masterpiece to last for all eternity.

February 4, 2015

Oh my, what a picture of dependence God placed upon my life! Was just talking to a good friend yesterday about desiring to understand more about really relying upon God in a resting sort of way when trials come. I tend to focus on the gap between my ability and what is needed, rather than God's desire and ability to fill it. Been asking Him to give me wisdom.

Well … Wisdom came in an odd, not so pleasant way last night. Out of the blue, my back went out and I was marooned holding onto the bottom bannister of our stairs. Only by pushing up on something with my arms could I get relief from the pain. Mark finally rescued me and by taking very small steps and putting all the pressure I could on Mark's hands could I move to a place where I could sort of rest. I now have a walker to use while I'm in this acute stage. If I do not use the weight of my hands to hold the pressure off my spine, then the pain escalates.

Another sweet friend who is a physical therapist came and worked on my back for hours last night and helped me set up my bed downstairs in the living room and help me learn how to move in the safest way. She spent the whole night on my couch to help me.

Hopefully time will heal all this. But it did strike me this morning that God has given me quite a powerful illustration of what He is and is not asking of me in learning to rely upon Him. It is not a matter of relying upon Him until I'm strong enough to rely upon myself – like something I graduate from. It's relying on His strength with every step in my weakness as I am right now.

He provided for me last night in remarkable ways, through my husband and this friend. And in another friend today sitting here with me as my spotter when I have to move. But most of all, behind it all there is Him, like the walker. Not waiting for me to get strong, but being my strength that I must rely upon every step of the way.

February 10, 2015
There's a world of difference in how you view your circumstances and God that stems from your understanding of what He is doing in this life.

Last Tuesday my back went out and since then it's been the ole MRI, doctor, ice, rest and meds routine. The issue once more confirmed to be this rare-ish condition called arachnoiditis, that is better described by what it isn't than what it is. The hardest part is that the doctor says it is unpredictable when I might have more of these debilitating episodes. I have a long way to go but am grateful for seeing the improvement I have. Sometimes with this condition you don't get all better. It has a tendency to worsen. This has been hard to process.

I realize that I still somehow have hopes for this being my 'best – or at least easiest – life now.' And weeks like this past one and whatever is still ahead put big cracks in this dream. I am still pretty much bed-ridden, though the pain is better and when I do get up to walk it's less painful, too. But, we don't know exactly how much better I will get or how long it will take. So, once more I'm bumping up against my view of God as I go through difficulties.

But I've been thinking … If you view this life as the place of God's greatest blessings, shown through easy days, good times or at least conquerable difficulties, then God doesn't seem good or make sense when you get hit with storm after storm. His hand is hard to see and His heart looks even harder. Why won't it stop? When will the sun come out and shine?

But, if we remember that Jesus promised that in this world we would have trouble. That our bodies are broken down, temporary dwellings, more like cardboard boxes than galvanized steel. If we can get past the huge bummer that, yes, all of our paths walk along, and eventually through, the valley of the shadow of death, then we can begin to see a whole new world of God's goodness and kind providences.

Instead of being mad at Him for us having to take the trail along the valley of the shadow of death, (as if there is any other path for frail humanity to take!), He can lift our eyes to see other, much more wonderful things, that are just as true of our trail.

Every day He provides what is needed. In front of us, He leaves the porch light of His promises on. His Spirit and His Word whisper to our hearts of His grand purposes, of His inability to waste our sorrows, and of the perfections of the life to come with Him … when all pain will be over, all wisdom and beauty of His plan revealed, and our hearts will be filled with His love to overflowing.

Seems to me we have a choice: to keep ourselves busy obsessing/avoiding/dreading the fact we are on the path that runs through the valley of the shadow of death, or we can recognize it, accept it and begin to appreciate how God has lined the whole way with His abundant goodnesses.

As hard as this week has been and as uncertain the road ahead still looks right now in terms of my back, I'm so grateful to be His child. I'm so grateful for the overflowing kindnesses He has shown me in so many ways. I'm so grateful that He will never leave me but carry me all the way home.

> Even to your old age, I am he. And to gray hairs
> I will carry you. I have made, and I will bear;
> I will carry and will save. ISAIAH 46:4

> Though I walk through the valley of the
> shadow of death I will fear no evil for you are
> with me. From PSALM 23

February 13, 2015

Wanted to thank everyone for praying. My back is improving! Able to walk more without aid of a walker, etc. Hopeful that this is going to heal up. Yay!

February 13, 2015

> Fight the good fight of the faith. Take hold of the
> eternal life to which you were called when you
> made your good confession in the presence of
> many witnesses. 1 TIMOTHY 6:12

I am so encouraged by this verse! It reminds me that victory in this life looks like a fight, not so much like 'arrival'. And, that this fight is a GOOD fight. It's worth every punch and bruise. It's worth every re-match of my old enemies, even if it's most every day. Why? Because it's the good fight of faith! It is taking hold of the eternal life, not just that we have received, as I usually think. But to which we are CALLED. In other words, while we taste bits of eternal life in our relationship with God right now, we are headed to the full inheritance of it that lies ahead in heaven. And, this good fight today is part of preparing us to know and receive all that is coming. So instead of being overwhelmed as the alarm clock sounds the bell on what seems like the start of Round 5000, we can put on our gloves and rejoice that today's fight doesn't just lead to victory, but is victory.

February 14, 2015

> My heart overflows with a pleasing theme; I address
> my verses to the king; my tongue is like the pen of a
> ready scribe. You are the most handsome of the sons
> of men; Grace is poured upon your lips; therefore
> God has blessed you forever. PSALM 45:1-2

A great prayer for the day! A tongue like the pen of a ready scribe. Engaged. Listening. Looking. Yearning to broadcast what comes from an overflowing heart.

This psalm is subtitled, *A love song.*

I guess this is what a Valentine's Day note to The Lord looks like.

February 15, 2015

> It is true that God's people are tested, but it is also true
> that God's grace is equal to their trials. SPURGEON

God's grace will always be equal to our trials because it is the sign and the servant of His faithfulness. God has promised to be faithful to His people forever. To not give grace would to be unfaithful. He cannot, He will not, act out of character. We can never 'out need' God. His faithfulness will always 'out give' our need. His grace will always trump whatever we require. Astounding!

February 16, 2015

Was thinking how my faith in God's providence gets tripped up on looking for the how's, when's and little why's of His plans: WHEN will something happen, HOW will He do it, WHY is He doing this right now? But God rarely gives those, so they make a very sparse diet. We can either go hungry, feed off of the wrong things, such as the passing securities and pleasures of this world ...

OR go feed on the right food He has given us ...

His 'will's' and His big 'why's'. He promised, so He WILL do it. And WHY can we count on Him to do what He promised ... and for it to all be for good? Because He sealed His promises with His Son's blood. Nothing can be more sure!

For God's people, it's never about what they deserve. It's about what God chose for them to receive because of what His Son deserves. All is ours because of who we are in Him.

To make things even better, is the fact that He WANTS to do this! He loves to give us all we need! He loves to be our protector and provider.

If anyone had the right to be 'mysterious' in what He's up to, it is God. He is that good. He is that wise. He is that infinite. He loves us that much!

February 18, 2015

> Let not a wise man boast of his wisdom, and let not
> the mighty man boast of his might, let not a rich
> man boast of his riches; but let him who boasts
> boast of this, that he understands and knows Me,
> that I am the Lord who exercises lovingkindness,
> justice, and righteousness on earth; for I delight in
> these things ... JEREMIAH 9:23-24 NAS.

My prayer for the day: to understand and know the Lord.

For Him to use everything in my day to better understand Him and know Him. To see, either by its face-value or by faith, that everything He does is purely out of loving kindness, justice and righteousness. And to be willing to wait for that which can now only be seen by faith to ripen into face-value in God's perfect, and usually much more patient time-frame.

Can you imagine having such a deep understanding and know of Him that it would be boast worthy? That's something worth asking Him for!

February 19, 2015

We may feel like we may need to run away from our troubles to find rest and safety, but with God, His loving strength keeps us safe out in the storm. His love is more than we can get our heads around. His power is greater than any foe. Nothing can touch us in any way but what He has chosen. ... And He is extremely protective about His children!

'With Christ in the vessel, we can smile at the storm, as we go sailing home.' – a bit of a kid's song we used to sing in the UK.

February 19, 2015

OK I can't resist! One more word picture for the day!

The playground here at our church has this funny suspended bridge feature that is both the terror and delight of the kids. It is made of planks of wood which have sturdy chains of metal that run through the middle of them in three places. This makes them both securely in place yet really wobbly as well. There are hand rails on both sides, too.

When you step on this bridge it does not feel very secure. It makes a wobbly noise and it moves under your feet. It feels like it's not sturdy enough to take you safely across from one side to the other. But it is.

Watching a child step on this bridge for the first time, you can see on their face the transition from terror to delight. Terror in the first few steps as they feel the wobble... But then delight as they see that they have balance enough to stay upright and the handrail to help them. They begin to relax and actually enjoy the wobbliness. They cross the bridge with growing confidence each time. It wobbles but they are safe. Now they can enjoy it.

I was just looking across the parking lot at that bridge and thinking that's how life feels at times. A noisy kind of wobbly and that shifts under your feet. Nothing much feels sturdy enough to take you safely across from one side to another. You wonder how you will manage.

But the more I cross the wobbly bits of the path God had given me, I find that each time I'm safe! God is like the handrail on the side and the strong chains underneath. I am safe even as I wobble! This is a controlled wobble. HIS controlled wobble. Not controlled by me, but by Him. He makes sure of that.

The more I realize this, the more my fears can be dropped and I can cross the wobbles with rest and even delight. With Him, we don't need to fear falling. We can enjoy the whole thing. He will provide. He will be our balance. He will hold us fast. And it will be amazing to see how He does it all.

February 22, 2015

Just listened to Mark's sermon from last Sunday and so convicted! How much I still long for what he describes as the Pharisee lifestyle. Want what I want now and want it to be easy. The thought of dodging my daily 'cross' is still so alluring, especially these days, when my body keeps throwing curve balls at me. I would be tempted to think God is being unkind to me for allowing thing after thing after thing to happen. But … I can see how much I need these trials in my heart. I have such resolve to be self-reliant. These trials cast me upon God day after day.

Like a little bonsai tree, He is clipping day after day with great precision and a particular shape in mind. He is good and right to send these struggles in a pretty unrelenting way. Doesn't mean I like them. Doesn't mean I feel particularly skilled at handling them. Actually am amazed at how bankrupt and beginner-ish I still am. Would even question my salvation, based on how bad I still am at all of this … But for one thing … God knew what I was like and saved me. His free gift in Jesus. He calls those in need to come to Him, not those who have it all together.

He says whoever comes to Him He will never turn away. I may not be doing much else, I may not be moving very quickly or very admirably. But I am coming to Him. And that gives me great hope.

He says He disciplines those He loves. Surely this is what is behind this crazy season.

February 23, 2015

> If any of you lacks wisdom, let him ask God, who gives generously to all without reproach, and it will be given him. JAMES 1:5

I love this promise! I have seen The Lord answer this promise over and over again. I used to pull it out in times when I needed … Well … Wisdom … Or should I say guidance about should I do this or that.

But lately, I've been learning that whatever I'm going through, to stop and ask myself: 'what do I need God to tell me or show me?' Then asking wisdom for that. Doing this helps me to get to the bottom of the heart struggle behind the situation. Things I would not have thought as wisdom issues really are. I can pray, 'God show how to trust you more … or …. God show how to flee temptation in a particular situation, etc.'

But I'm also learning that while I used to think of God giving wisdom as kind of asking for advice, I realize that a lot of times, God's giving wisdom to me is through what He brings to my life. Not so much show by telling as show through training me. It may not feel like He's giving me wisdom at first, but really there are just so many times when we only can learn something by doing rather than just hearing what needs to be done.

So grateful that God is faithful to always show us the way to go and help us to get there. He knows just what He's doing!

February 23, 2015

So friends, I really need you to pray. Friday I developed what has now been identified as an unusual reaction to the thyroid med I am on. It makes me tremble and I feel so jittery that it's like I'm on an IV of caffeine. They are hoping to try something else tomorrow. But for now I am not in good shape at all. This is almost unbearable. Would you please pray that this reaction subside? And … That the new med would not cause this same reaction. It's so tough bc I have to have some form of thyroid to live since I have none of my own. But I cannot imagine enduring this either. Thank you so much for praying!

February 23, 2015

Wanted to say that The Lord is answering our prayers! My body has calmed down considerably. I think I will be able to even sleep tonight! So grateful! New Meds come in tomorrow at noon. Ugh! We will see what we get! Thanks again for caring and if you think of it, would appreciate you to pray over the next few days. Mark is out of town for ten days starting on Wed. Hate to have him gone while I go through this. But … My sweet daughter-in-law is coming to be with me. Yay for that!

February 24, 2015

6 a.m. and thanks to a merciful God and kind friends I've gotten at least sleep off and on. Thank you! Please do pray

for this new med! The thought of putting another pill in my mouth that may cause this reaction to start up in full force again is frankly terrifying. But I'm going to have to do it around 1 my time this afternoon. I would rather have the reaction while Mark is still here. But my muscles are trembling partly as leftover from the reaction and partly bc I'm so scared of what may happen next. Just so grateful to know that though I may not see the path, that there is one there and God will lead me along. Oh but I am scared ...

February 24, 2015
From Psalm 16:

> Preserve me, oh God, for in you I take refuge. I say to the Lord, 'you are my Lord; I have no good apart from you.' ... The Lord is my chosen portion and my cup; you hold my lot. The lines have fallen for me in pleasant places; indeed, I have a beautiful inheritance. I bless the Lord who gives me counsel; in the night also my heart instructs me. I have set the Lord always before me; because he is at my right hand, I shall not be shaken. Therefore my heart is glad, and my whole being rejoices; my flesh also dwells secure. For you will not abandon my soul to Sheol, or let your holy once the corruption. You make known to me the path of life; in your presence there is fullness of joy; at your right hand are pleasures forever more.

Good to have such wonderful promises to sink into. The boundaries that feel like a strait jacket are only temporary in the grand scheme of things. And, will one day be seen to be the cords of love that they always were. He gives me this promise now. And kindly comforted me through you all and His unshakeable promises.

February 24, 2015

My new med came in too late today to start it so tomorrow a.m. will begin. Oh how nice it was not to have that terrible reaction today! And who knows, maybe the new Meds will be OK. Hope so. Thanks for praying! Really appreciate the support!

February 25, 2015

Update for those praying …

Took med at 2:50 when my muscle pain and body heaviness from being hypo thyroid for thirty-six hours. Got too awful to even lay down. Think it may be a better fit med in the long run but the dose is way too high. Extremely jittery. Fine tremors all over my body. Awful to just ride this out. Please pray the doctor will lower the dose immediately when I call. Please pray for it to calm down and for me to bear this somehow.

> Oh my strength I will watch for you for you oh God
> are my fortress my God in his steadfast love will
> meet me. PSALM 59: 9,10 ESV

February 25, 2015

Thank you so much for praying me through this today!!! I need your help!

Jitters gone now back to this extreme heaviness can hardly stand up. Tongue even heavy. Hard to speak as normal. Please pray. Message left for doctor waiting to hear back.

I know some of you deal with hypothyroidism. Is this what it feels like?

February 25, 2015
Last update! Thanks again for caring!

Endocrinologist said to see my GP. Just saw her. She was actually fantastic and spent an hour with me! Lots of bloodwork ordered. They believe my levels are so messed up … Electrolytes etc especially the calcium. Hopefully they can help me find out what is out of whack and gradually get me better. Wow! What a wild ride this last year has been!

March 1, 2015

> The time that the people of Israel lived in Egypt was 430 years. At the end of 430 years, on that very day, all the hosts of the Lord went out from the land of Egypt. It was a night of watching by the Lord, to bring them out of the land of Egypt. Exodus 12:40-42

Two things I love about this passage.

#1. To the day … 430 years to the day
The Lord knew exactly what He was doing and exactly how long it would last. He had planned it to be 430 years in Egypt and so it was. There were some good years at the beginning, then many difficult years. But each one was numbered by the day. I love that the Lord is so in control! His plans are so certain!

#2. It was a night of watching by the Lord
That's so wonderful! Not only had He planned the day of deliverance but He brought it Himself. Not a general

mindfulness, a general plan, but perhaps a distant God. No, God hires no nannies. God is on duty! He stands watch. He knows His plans and He, Himself, brings them about. He is with His people.

March 1, 2015

> Blessed are they that hunger and thirst for righteousness for they shall be filled. MATTHEW 5:6

We need food, whether or not we are hungry for it. When it comes to our bodies, we are all too willing to eat, whether or not we feel hunger. (Perfect example are the gluten free donut holes I had this morning! Yum!). But there's no doubting it, when we are hungry, we look for a way to fill it. Incentive is high!

How even more true with spiritual hunger and food. We may eat whether we feel our hunger or not. And this is good. But when we do hunger, we seek out food. There's nothing like a 'bare cupboard' to make you hunger for what you don't have and make you wonder where it will come from.

I suppose that's why when God goes about making a meal plan for us, He includes emptiness and difficulty as 'appetizers'. They create the appetite for what He next wants to feed us. He is both creator and ruler over the hunger and the food with which He will satisfy the hunger. The two go together beautifully for God's amazing purposes. The hunger is as great a part of God's gift to us as the being filled part. I certainly am hungry for a pretty different set of things for God to do in my heart than before all this started over a year ago. I can't say I have enjoyed the hunger process, but I know I've needed it. And, I'm grateful for how He's changed my appetite. A lot more filling and eating to be done. But realizing that He is behind the hunger, creating it and allowing it in order to fill me is so encouraging.

> He humbled you, causing you to hunger, feeding you with manna, that neither you nor your fathers did know, that He might make you know that man does not live by bread alone, but on every word that comes from the mouth of God. DEUTERONOMY 8:3

March 3, 2015

> But, as it is written, 'What no eye has seen, nor ear heard, nor the heart of man imagined, what God has prepared for those who love him.' 1 CORINTHIANS 2:9

> Oh, the depth of the riches and wisdom and knowledge of God! How unsearchable are his judgments and how inscrutable his ways! ROMANS 11:33

Thinking about the world of difference between 'incredible' and 'incomprehensible'.

Incredible is another way of saying 'I don't believe it.' Incomprehensible is another way of saying 'I don't understand it.'

So much of God's ways are more than we can understand. He is infinite and we have but pea-sized brains. He is up to plans the length of eternity and we just barely have focus for a day's worth of life. We too often stand off, more like strangers to Him, when He would have us draw closer.

At least for me, the difference between what God is up to and what I can understand leads me to a choice each day: will it be incredulity or incomprehensibility?

Will I head towards unbelief and judgment because everything doesn't make sense or His promises seem too big to possibly be true?

Or will I head towards trusting in the Lord and humbly admitting my inability to understand? Acknowledging me to be small and Him and His ways to be good and so big that they are incomprehensible ... at least for now?

> Immediately the father of the child cried out and said, 'I believe; help my unbelief!' MARK 9:24

> Trust in the Lord with all your heart and do not lean on your own understanding. In all your ways acknowledge Him and He will make your paths straight. PROVERBS 3:5-6

March 5, 2015

> And when the dew had gone up, there was on the face of the wilderness a fine, flake-like thing, fine as frost on the ground. When the people of Israel saw it, they said to one another, 'what is it?' for they did not know what it was. And Moses said to them, 'it is the bread that the Lord has given you to eat'. EXODUS 16:14

Looking for the bread from heaven to be fed upon in the wilderness of this day. He promises it to us. And if it comes in a 'what is it' form, asking for God to provide the wise counselor to help me identify it as the food He intends it to be. And, asking for a humble spirit that isn't scared off by or grumbly about the wilderness-ishness of the day. Just going to wait expectantly for His promised provision.

March 6, 2015

Continuing to think about that manna off and on all day today. A new thought came to mind about it: God could have created manna as a food type when He created the world, but He didn't. He held off and saved it for this one, special forty years of history. That's it. Of all the years of this world, only forty years for a particular people – His people – did He bring forth manna.

What else has He held back from this world that He could bring out to rescue or sustain His people in times of need? He is the creator of the universe out of nothing but His Word. Will we faithlessly limit Him to only what we see and know when we need rescuing?

And even more amazing, who knows what other things He has held back from this current world and is saving for the new heaven and earth to come? What an exciting home He has gone to prepare for us and will bring us to one day!

March 6, 2015

> Your eyes saw my unformed substance; in your
> book were written, every one of them, the days
> that were formed for me, when as yet there was
> none of them. PSALM 139:16

Perhaps God's book in which the days of His people's lives are written is a picture book.

God's promises and mercies are new every morning. They are like the golden frame around a blank canvas. His hand works each day, painting in the daily picture the specifics of His faithful outworkings of those promises and that mercy. Each day we can look as He fills in the masterpiece He creates specifically for us, custom-made for this one day.

The hues may be brighter one day and darker the next. The subject in focus may vary. But every one will bear His particular style every bit as much as a Rembrandt always looks like a Rembrandt. He will always be faithful. He will always provide enough. He will always be loving us and merciful to us. Always bearing us towards home. That is what it's all about. A display of His glory here. A life in His glory there.

March 10, 2015

Today was in fact one of the most battle-torn days that I have had in a long time … And that is saying a lot, since many days of this past year have not been easy. But today was like a field of sinking sandpits and I kept hitting one after another of the big kinds of things that trigger my fears. It was absolutely horrendous … And I got whupped. Praise God for friends who prayed for me as I fought!

But … I must say while I did little but writhe and fight against my fears all day and not in a particularly pretty way … While I felt assaulted and overwhelmed with my weakness in light of the raging battle, I must say that I know I need this. I don't want it, but I need it. I still hold so tightly into the wrong things. Battles like today show how much my reliance needs to be less on the pretty props I've come to love and more on our steadfast God. They are all just dust in the wind. All but Him.

So with Job, I must say. 'Though He slay me, yet will I praise Him.'

I waited patiently for the Lord. He turned to me
when I called. He lifted me out of the slimy pit; out
of the muck and mire. He put my feet on a rock. He
gave me a firm place to stand. He put a new song in
my heart, a hymn of praise to my God. PSALM 40

It is no easy matter to bring a man from nature to grace,
and from grace to glory, so unyielding and intractable
are our hearts. How kindly and gently God's hand
works even in the gale-force winds of struggle that may
blow. RICHARD SIBBES *The Bruised Reed*

March 15, 2015

Praising the Lord today, for His promises to turn the land
mines of our lives into gold and diamond mines.

Count it all joy, my brothers, when you meet trials of
various kinds, for you know that the testing of your faith
produces steadfastness. And let steadfastness have its
full effect, that you may be perfect and complete, lacking
in nothing. JAMES 1:2-4

March 17, 2015

If this past year has taught me (the beginnings of) anything
about a Christian's growth towards God, it is that the
process is one of the blacksmith's forge.

Our desires for change are like sketches of what we want
God to do. But nine times out of ten, our steely hearts must
feel the heat of difficulty and the sparks must fly, for God to
actually work the change we desire within us.

I keep wanting the changes to come easily or automati-
cally, but I realize that God keeps sending me trials, at least

in part, in order to answer my prayers to love Him and fear Him more. It seems to be the only way, at least with my heart!

We can't be pleased with this painful prospect unless we set as our goal for Christ to be formed in us.

And for that to be our goal of choice is only a work of God's Spirit within us. There's simply nothing in this world that would make us want to ask God to work in us, knowing full well that it's trials that work this wonder.

But … gulp … Let us continue to ask God for this! Let us continue to set our eyes on the unseen, inconceivably wonderful prize of fullness of joy in the presence of God forever!

> Though our private desires are ever so confused, though our private requests are ever so broken, and though our private groanings are ever so hidden from men, yet God eyes them, records them, and puts them upon the file of heaven, and will one day crown them with glorious answers and returns. THOMAS BROOKS

March 22, 2015

Do you ever wish you needed a little less grace? Do you ever wish you could just get things right in your own strength and by your own good efforts? That the 'Well, done good and faithful servant' words that Christ will bless us with when we see Him would be a bit more about our own faithfulness and fruitfulness for Him … instead of simply through Him? I certainly do! I'm amazed at how many times I think I've done something well and squeaky-clean good to later see how much it had the filthy rags of my unrighteousness in it. And, to see God still use what I've done, but in His own ways and actually in spite of me instead of because of me. Ah, He is the potter and we are very much just clay.

I know that we are called to do God's will the best we can; and, to do it wisely, godly and hopefully fruitfully. But, I'm wondering what really is the most important element to being a good and faithful servant? And, what is the most important fruit to bear? What if it was the willingness, humility, dependence and contentment of my heart rather than buckets of output? God has given each of us different gifts and has planned each day of our lives. Therefore what God requires of us, in terms of output, will not, cannot, should not, look the same for all of us. But those other things, those things of the heart. Now there the playing field levels out. Willingness, humility, dependence, contentment, we are all called to these. That sounds like clay waiting to be shaped for God's purposes. Praying for this servant heart today.

March 23, 2015
'The Lord is my shepherd I shall not want.' PSALM 23:1

We do not need to fear what lies ahead, not because it will be easy or predictable or we are strong. We do not need to fear because of who it is who leads the way, who has chosen the path, and knows just what He's doing.

We are but sheep with but sheeply brains. No wonder we don't understand. We just don't have the capacity to take it all in. Lacking the capacity to understand, we have two choices: to fear because we don't understand ... or to lean upon God's understanding and find rest.

Oh, to fight to lean and rest today!

March 27, 2015

I don't know about you, but I detect a definite sliding scale of what I like to receive from God. I love for Him to give me gifts of strength and blessing, skills and success. These are the peach cobbler and ice cream of my life. Yum! Can't get enough of them. But also have to admit … There's room for a ton of self-sufficiency and God-forgetfulness here.

Then next on the scale come strength and grace for my weakness. There is the pit of the stomach groan here, as it is obvious that I cannot, on my own, do what is needed. And, only if God acts, will it happen. But even in this part of the scale, there is the beauty and excitement of partnership, of fellowship with God. And, there is a bit of dignity in weakness: 'I would if I could, but I can't-ness' to it. 'Ah, look at the poor thing limping along but trying.' Yes … Trying … There is still a bit of self-something or other here.

And then there comes the far end of the scale. The dark side. My sin. My rebellion. Now here I don't like to look very much. I don't like to see how much is there. I don't like to see its stark, towering shape. And I really don't like the fact that there is nothing in me that I can muster up to somehow imagine I deserve God's rescuing forgiveness. There is all of shame and not an ounce of deserving left here.

But it's here where the real depths of God's love can be known and received. God forgives sinners. God loves sinners who turn to him. There is something exceedingly wonderful about a love that asks for no deserving but covers all just the same.

Every day I need to visit all parts of this scale. Take joy and use the good gifts God has given. Ask for strength for my weakness. And to remember the depths of my true identity: a sinner saved and freed to truly live because of my Savior who shed His blood for my sins.

> But God demonstrates his own love for us in
> this: While we were still sinners, Christ died
> for us. ROMANS 5:8

March 31, 2015

> For all the promises of God find their Yes in him.
> That is why it is through him that we utter our Amen
> to God for his glory. 2 CORINTHIANS 1:20

I love spring flowers and blooming trees, but I loved them perhaps most this year when I first saw the tips of their shoots and the bulges of their buds declare war on this long, long winter. None of the beautiful color yet, but all of the promise. Spring is coming! Winter will end! Take heart!

Perhaps I loved them most like this because they best echo the defiance God's promises hold out to me in my present weariness of body, mind and spirit. This next week I will have multiple appointments and tests that will help chart the course ahead with cancer related matters. Winter feels like it is hanging on. But God has filled His Word with wonderful promises of His perfect care down to the every detail. The shoots and the buds are showing. They point hopefully to His goodness and mercy for every day on this journey to His house where He is preparing a place for me! Every foot step is plotted out with loving sovereignty.

April 4, 2015

> All the days ordained for me were written in your
> book before one of them came to be. PSALM 139:16
>
> I do not write my own story; it has been written
> for me. My job is to live inside of the plot that God
> has written for me in the way I have been called by
> Him to live ...
>
> Do you question God's administration of your
> story? Do you wish that you had been able to write
> your own plot? Do you fall into thinking that if you
> had been in charge, you would've made better and
> wiser choices? ...
>
> Do you worship God as sovereign on Sunday and
> curse His sovereignty on Tuesday? As you look back
> on your life, is it more a picture of resting in His
> control or of a quest for your control?
>
> God is sovereign. You and I are not. This is not
> just theology; it is our identity. God is in absolute
> control, and He is infinitely good.
>
> PAUL DAVID TRIPP from his book *Lost in the Middle*

This past week I have definitely felt lost in the middle. Yes,
middle, as in middle-age I guess you could say, since I'm fifty-
four. But also lost in the middle of the fears of unknowns
with this cancer stuff and what these next appointments
and tests will say.

And lost in the middle of the unknowns that lay not just
with this cancer but in so many other areas of my life. I am
deeply appreciative to Paul Tripp for writing this book. It has
been so helpful for me to see that the deepest, biggest, real-est
struggle going on right now has very little to do with cancer or

the handful of other 'burrs' of daily life that are pricking me. Nope. The real issue is the struggle for me to be happy on my own terms rather than finding contentment, resting in God and His wise and sometimes mysterious plans instead. Tripp helps me see the root for what it is. I'm grateful!

Oh, terrible fight! Oh, wonderful God! That lets me toss and turn in my own willfulness in a way that leads me – I think – ultimately to the peace that passes understanding and surpasses every trial.

April 5, 2015

> And this is eternal life, that they know you the only true God, and Jesus Christ whom you have sent. JOHN 17:3

If eternal life is most of all knowing God and knowing Him more and more through all eternity, then that makes today, perhaps more than anything else, a part of that unfolding.

Everything we go through is chosen to help us know Him more. There is nothing risky, in the sense that God will forsake us or not be able to bring about the one, best outcome that He planned for every event that His dear children go through. There are only opportunities to see His steadfast love and goodness. We may fear, but we need not fear.

God, how do you want to show yourself to me today? Help me turn from being so caught up in the situation that I miss and fail to grow from what you want me to see, enjoy and rest in about You. You are the greatest gift of the day.

April 7, 2015

Would you please pray? My big cancer check-up appointment is Thursday and to be honest, I slept very little last night and continue to be fighting the jitters even now. They will check my blood work, get some other test results, check a few little lymph nodes that hopefully will turn out to be nothing, and set up my radioactive iodine scan and other possible tests.

Please pray that I would enjoy today and push off prying into Thursday and possible outcomes. Please pray for me to lean into God's everlasting arms and His ability to carry, to save, to love and to strengthen me. I am weak, but He is strong. I want to be a display of confidence in how wonderful He is.

And ... If you would please pray for a full day of recording after a night of almost no sleep. Thank you friends!

LAMENTATION 3:22

April 9, 2015

Thanks for your prayers and encouragements! The doctor said the lymph nodes I was worried about were fine! Yay! The bloodwork of consequence still wasn't in yet. Ultrasound tomorrow and then radioactive iodine scan in about month. So yay for what was good and back to waiting and learning through waiting. Well ... Trying to learn through waiting. I'm still so bad at waiting with a quiet heart. Thanks again for caring!

April 9, 2015

My husband sent this quote to me. Thought I would share it with you:

> 'What cannot be cured must be endured.' I am
> afraid I have often said it, but when I have done

so it was because for the moment I have forgotten my Christianity. 'What cannot be cured must be endured' is paganism. It is wonderful that paganism ever climbed to that height. It is a great attitude, it is heroic up to a certain point, but it is not Christianity.

Christianity does not say 'what cannot be cured must be endured.' It says, rather, 'These things must be endured because they are part of the cure.' These things are to be cheerfully borne because they have the strange and mystic power to make whole and strong, and so lead to victory and the final glory.

Christianity is never the dour pessimism which submits. Christianity is the cheerful optimism which cooperates with the process, because it sees that through suffering and weakness, joy and strength come ...

Look back over the years. There they are, travel-worn years; much of light is upon them, but much of darkness also; many days of triumph, with the band playing and the flags flying, and many days of disaster and defeat.

Already you know that the greatest things of life have not come out of the sunlit days, but out of darkened hours. Your sorrow has already been turned into joy. When your sorrow, that which was unendurable as it seemed at that hour, blossomed with beauty, your sorrow was turned into joy.

Christianity, as an experience, is the ability to know that this will be so, even while the agony is upon us, and so we are able to sing in the midst of it. Men who sing while they suffer are men who have learned the profound secret that suffering is the

method by which is perfected human life
and history.

> G. Campbell Morgan, quoted in
> In The Shadow of Grace, pp. 62-63.

April 12, 2015

From *The Hardest Peace* by Kara Tippetts, a young woman who just recently died after an amazing struggle with illness:

> Miraculously, my story had the freedom to be
> changed. I was able to turn over the authorship of
> my story to the One who knew how to best write
> my life. I could trust again, knowing the story wasn't
> promised to be easy, but I was no longer silent in it.
> I was a beautifully redeemed daughter of the King.
> I would walk in grace.

And …

> I have had so many surgeries. Under my clothes I look
> like a science experiment. But I am no longer the
> scared little girl who struggled for love. No, I enter
> the scary and hard looking for grace, expecting grace,
> with face lifted, walking in love unimaginable. Life is
> not as I dreamed it would be all those years ago. In
> many ways, it's far beyond those dreams.

The thing I love the most about what Kara writes is about entering the hard and scary looking for grace and expecting grace. We all will face many hardships in life. I am so grateful that as a believer in Jesus, that my whole life with all the sufferings, will have God's story on them. Everything will be all for my good as well as His glory. There WILL be grace for each day. I can bank on that. How wonderful!

April 15, 2015

Dear friends, I got the results back from my doctor. Unfortunately they were not clear as we had hoped. The markers in my blood work did not go down as they should. And ultrasound showed up two thyroid nodules and one lymph node which all need further investigation. (How do you even have thyroid nodules when they took your thyroid out! I guess thyroid cancer cells is what they think.) None of these were there back in November when I had my last ultrasound.

The doctor mentioned a number of things which might be ahead. Maybe radiation, maybe surgery, maybe wait-and-see. It all depends on the next two new things they've added in before my scan: attempted biopsies of the three spots and a special injection which will tell them more about my cancer marker. Those will be coming a week from Friday and a week from Monday. I've been stunned, sad and now today the ugh and panic of it all has begun to hit. I was so hoping that this was done. Fear is trying to take complete control.

But had a wonderful weekend up in the mountains. How can we look at a computer or car and appreciate the great mind and works of man, yet look at the mountains and not appreciate the far greater mind and works of God! His greatness is all around us in the seen world. His Word and His Spirit tell us of the even greater workings of Him in the unseen world. The storm is furious. I feel disoriented. But God's plans stand firm. He will guide. He will carry. He will! He will!

Sure would appreciate your prayers. Grace for each day and eyes focused on today and eternity.

April 15, 2015

As I'm learning to expect God's gifts of grace for the day, two things seem to happen. Life becomes a bit like one of those 'I Spy' pictures, crammed full of stuff and you are supposed to find certain objects they list. You know they are there. Just keep looking for them!

A treasure hunt of God's goodness and mercy that He promises to His children for every day of their lives.

And, it seems that when I get busy looking for His grace, it pushes me off center stage and puts Him there instead. Life is always better when God is in the spotlight! Maybe His reflected grace in our lives can be like little spotlights that make Him more clearly seen!

April 16, 2015

Boy, this is hard! I so don't know what I'm doing! These are new, unfamiliar lands. Shepherd, pick me up and carry me!

April 16, 2015

Wanted to thank you for your prayers! God was so mighty in answering them! Was up for hours in the night but then today had a remarkably normal day in which I was able to see people and be productive in a way I would have not thought even imaginable. I'm so so grateful for all of your prayers and God answering them as He did today! Thank you!!!!

April 18, 2015

When Jesus tells us to become like little children, He isn't telling us to do anything He isn't already doing. Jesus is, without question, the most dependent

182

human being who ever lived ... He prays and He
prays and He prays.
A Praying Life by PAUL E. MILLER

Jesus' dependence upon the Father was fueled by a love and deep intimacy with Him. His 'I can do nothing without the Father' was the reflection of perfect humanity. It was an expression of His position of choice in life. This is deeply who He was and is.

God calls us to this position in our lives, too. But it seems that at least the rebelliousness of my not-so-pure heart makes dependence upon God feel like a crisis too many times. And the less there is within me or around me that I see as a resource that can be relied upon, the bigger the crisis.

The thorny brambles of doubt keep growing up across my path. Their sting has trained me to fear dependence upon God as risky. Unseen and unknown (by me) = unreliable.

But actually this is the very position God created us to live and to thrive. And, the more I ask for eyes to see His steadfast care and a mind to remember it, the more He gives me and the closer He draws me to Him.

No wonder He sends trials that strip us of our personal resources to cope. The position of dependence that Jesus knew and loved is one that all too often we must be pressured into. Funny, it's like God having to force-feed us birthday cake! He's wanting us to taste and see just how good He is! Trials are His nudges – and as necessary, even blows – of love, that He employs to bring us to Him. They are His cords of kindness that He will use, with all wisdom and gentleness, to bring us to intimacy with Him. How good and necessary is the Lord's discipline of His children!

April 24, 2015

A lot of needle action with no results today with my biopsies. They couldn't get the nodule to hold still and it was too close to the carotid artery and the trachea. But it's done and that's good! Next week the injections and the whole body scan which should be more helpful in painting the pic of what's going on … And what is needed.

Thanks so much for praying! It's been a good week in the new training God has me in. Basically, to stop thinking about how will I get strong enough to do what is the next hard thing. Instead, to ask God for more grace to do whatever He wants me to do. I don't have to get stronger. I have to be more reliant … Let Him be stronger. He really has given me so much grace! Not grace in big lumps, like what I thought victory would look like. But in little teaspoons that I ask for again and again. I'm as bankrupt in myself as ever, but I'm growing in being confident of God's riches, graciously given.

Thanks again for praying!

A bruised reed shall He not break. ISAIAH 42:3

I was in to Jesus just to get my pain and my paralysis fixed. And I realize that yes, Jesus cares about suffering and He spent most of His time when He was on this earth relieving it. But the gospel of Mark showed me His priorities because the same man that healed blind eyes and withered hands is the same one who said, 'Gouge out that eye, cut off that hand if it leads you into sin.'

I got the picture. To me, physical healing had always been the big deal, but to God, my soul was a much bigger deal. And that's when I began searching for a deeper healing, not just a physical healing, although I was still praying for such. I asked for a deeper healing, a Psalm 139, 'Search me, O God, try my heart, test me and (singing) see if there be some wicked way in me. Cleanse me from every sin and set me free.'

And I tell you what, for the last forty-six years that's been my prayer. And God has been answering it, exposing things in my heart from which I need to be healed and I tell you what, I am so far from being finished, so far.

JONI EARECKSON TADA
A Deeper Healing / Grace to You

April 25, 2015

Be strong and courageous. Do not be dismayed before the King of Assyria and all the horde that is with him ... with him is an arm of flesh, but with us is the LORD our God, to help us and to fight our battles. 2 CHRONICLES 32:7-8

Wow! That was the biggest arm of flesh around in those days. The Israelites were way outnumbered, but the Lord did defeat them ... And without the people even lifting one finger. He did it while they were sleeping! This is the same God is who is with us today!

May 1, 2015

Just got back from scans! Scans looked pretty good. There is one something up near my voice box that they are trying to figure out. Will take blood work results and probably a CT scan to get a better idea. Right near voice box so that's tricky even if benign. Back to waiting but so very grateful for what wasn't there today … And very grateful for your love and prayers. Probably will hear from the doctor what will come next by the middle of next week.

May 2, 2015

> Come, Thou, fount of every blessing,
> Tune my heart to sing Thy praise,
> Streams of mercies, never-ceasing,
> Call for songs of loudest praise!
>
> ROBERT ROBINSON

Needing to focus on the fount of every blessing today, instead of just the blessings. Even the most abundant, seemingly un-movable, dependable blessings of my life are only blooms. Yesterday I received word that another close friend, very close friend, may be moving away. My next-door neighbor of twenty years is holding a yard sale before they move away. I hear it in the background as I work and it makes me sad. In the past year so many of my closest friends have left and most of the rest of them are contemplating a move in the near future. This, plus uncertainty about my health, just continues to remind me to not focus on the blessings that God has given me … but on the fount of the blessings. He will always be here. He will always give what is needed. I can let the people, the health, the dreams, the agenda, and everything else go as He has planned. This fount will never run dry. He will provide more even as He takes away. This means I can appreciate the blessings He gives me today without gripping them and making idols of them. Well… At least that's the prayer of my heart. Fortunately, He gives grace to do this, even where I find myself powerless. How good, how overflowingly able is our God!

May 16, 2015

> Blessed be the Lord, who daily bears us up; God is
> our salvation. PSALM 68:19

I love that the God who promises us eternal security and hope, understands that His frail people need to receive it not just as one big gulp, but as daily carries.

I know that I certainly need it as daily carries because I am forgetful and so prone to wander. I need to come back thirsty every day because I am all too willing to take the good gifts that He gives me here and make them towers of security. Daily helps keep that tendency a bit more unfulfilled.

Praise God for being a good father who gives us what we need, in the amounts we need, at just the time that we need it. Praise God for His wisdom in daily showing us how empty we are and in doing so, driving us to Him.

May 17, 2015

Here's a little update on things …

So my cancer blood marker is above the threshold for active cancer and is rising. Tomorrow I have a CT scan to check out the suspicious lump in my neck they noticed on the scan a few weeks ago. In June I'm scheduled for a special scan that tells them how much more radiation they can safely give me and plan to give that amount to me in late June. Then back in quarantine for a while after that. The only thing I don't know is whether they will move these things around to do surgery on the neck lump if it is cancer. If it's not cancer then they don't know where it is exactly but will treat me now before it grows more. It can become resistant to this kind of radiation so they want to use it before that happens.

I sure would appreciate your prayers as I go through this. Hoping for clarity on the scan tomorrow, for them not to overdose me on radiation so that my bone marrow and lungs can fully recover, and I long for both myself and all around me to see how true it is that there is a God in heaven. He is good and can be known ... Jesus is alive and to know Him and live for Him is better even than life. And yes ... I am scared.

May 17, 2015

OK ... So tonight is really, really hard. I'm really fighting fear of unknown right now. Panicking. Please pray that I give my God the greatest honor I can of not needing to know His will in order to feel safe and just delighting in Him and whatever He wants and has planned. Thank you!

May 20, 2015

> When my soul was embittered, when I was pricked in heart, I was brutish and ignorant; I was like a beast towards You. Nevertheless, I am continually with You; You hold my right hand. You guide me with your counsel, and afterword You will receive me to glory. Whom have I in heaven but you? And there is nothing on earth that I desire besides you. My flesh and my heart may fail, but God is the strength of my heart and my portion forever. PSALM 73:22-26

Loving Psalm 73 today! This is a real relationship between a real person who struggles with real things and even fights against the very real God that he loves. He is embittered. He admits that he is upset with God about some of the things he has to go through. He's probably even said things to God that he knows he shouldn't of said because he's just plain upset. It's not a particularly pretty sight.

And yet his God is as real as this man and his struggles are. This is no wimpy, flighty God. He is good and faithful even to His fussy, grumpy child. So even as he is upset, this man knows God is still with him continually. He knows He's holding onto his hand and giving him counsel. He knows that his wonderful loving God is leading him home to glory. He is confident that even when his flesh fails in death and as his heart feels torn with doubt at times, God is his strength. God is his portion. He belongs to God and God will never abandon him. What love is this, oh my soul! Who is like the Lord!

> Why should I feel discouraged? Why should the
>   shadows fall?
> Why should my heart keep longing, longing for
>   heaven and home?
> For Jesus is my portion. My constant friend is He.
> His eye is on the sparrow, and I know He watches
>   me!
>   Civilla D. Martin

May 27, 2015

> I will betroth you to me forever; I will betroth
> you in righteousness and justice, in love and
> compassion. Hosea 2:19

> For He has rescued us from the dominion of
> darkness and brought us into the kingdom of the

Son He loves, in whom we have redemption, the
forgiveness of sins. COLOSSIANS 3:13

Next week Mark and I get to celebrate thirty-three years of
marriage. So excited to spend a week up at this beautiful
place with him!

But more sure than even the sweet, steadfast, long-
suffering, generous love of my husband (especially exhibited
this past very difficult year), is the love God has shown
me. ... Through Mark, through wonderful friends, and
most of all through His choice of trials and blessings. He
truly is the one who has faithfully betrothed Himself to
us! Oh, to simply rest and delight in Him and His perfect,
husbandliness!

May 27, 2015

I just heard from my doctor regarding the CT scan I had
ten days ago. Nothing new came from the test as to where
the cancer is. So, we will proceed as planned. Six days of
scanning with small amount of radiation on June 8-15 to
calculate the biggest dose my body can safely take, then
administering the large dose on June 25th.

Only a few hospitals in the country do this special scan
to figure dosage so I'm very grateful to get it. But, there's
still quite a bit of guess work even with this.

There is a constant (at least) low level amount of appre-
hension I'm fighting every day just thinking about all of
this. I would certainly appreciate your prayers both for me
and for the doctors to choose the right level for my body.
Wanting to entrust myself fully into my loving Father's
plans. I so hope to deal with the radiation with no lasting

damage to anything but the cancer ... But I am His and want to bow humbly and trustingly even if He allows for something other than this. Thanks for your prayers and for caring!

May 27, 2015

Ugh! So I guess it's all hitting me what's coming. I'm pretty much 100% panicking. Would you please pray for grace for today to trust God and to not have to know outcomes in order to have peace? To lean into His purely good and loving character? Thanks so much!

May 27, 2015

God is hearing your prayers! Thank you so much! I'm doing better. Grateful! But certainly don't mind if you keep on holding me up in prayer. I am weak but He is strong!

May 31, 2015

Some quotes I'm mulling over from *Behind a Frowning Providence* by John Murray.

> People are usually more anxious to get rid of their problems than they are to find the purpose of God in them.

> Afflictions are continued no longer than till they have done their work. It is our responsibility to pray that our afflictions will be sanctified to us.

> A friend found herself in a sea of troubles. Attempting to encourage her, he said 'I want you to know that we are praying for you'. 'I appreciate

that,' she replied, 'what are you praying for God to do?' He found himself struggling for an answer and mentioned some things. 'Thank you,' she said, 'but please pray for one more request. Pray that I won't waste all the suffering.'

God moves in a mysterious way
His wonders to perform;
He plants His footsteps in the sea,
And rides upon the storm.

Deep in unfathomable mines
Of never failing skill
He treasures up His bright designs
And works His sovereign will.

You fearful saints, fresh courage take;
The clouds you so much dread
Are big with mercy, and shall break
In blessings on your head.

Judge not the Lord by feeble sense,
But trust Him for His grace;
Behind a frowning Providence
He hides a smiling face.

His purposes will ripen fast,
Unfolding every hour;
The bud may have a bitter taste,
But sweet will be the flower.

Not till the loom is silent
And the shuttle cease to fly
Shall God unroll the canvas
And explain the reason why.

The dark threads are as needful
in the weaver's skillful hand
As the threads of gold and silver
In the pattern He has planned.

Deep waters crossed life's path way;
The hedge of thorns was sharp;
Now these lie all behind me;
Oh! For a well-tuned harp!

Soon shall the cup of blessing
Wash down Earth's bitterest woes;
Soon shall the desert briar
Break into Eden's rose.

Blind unbelief is sure to err
And scan His work in vain;
God is His own interpreter,
And He will make it plain.

WILLIAM COWPER

May 31, 2015

If I could ask for one prayer for this next week it would be
that I would not be distracted by my health or fears or anything but bring smiling, fun, even light-hearted delight to my
husband as we get to spend Monday through Saturday down
at wintergreen. Tears have been an almost daily companion
lately. This would such a sweet gift as the last thing before all
the radiation stuff begins. Thank you so much for praying!

June 2, 2015

Sufferings drive us to God. We set out in service
thinking God needs us. We soon find out that we need

Him. When God lays men on their backs, then they look up to heaven. We cry to God for blessings but we do not really want Him. He has to teach us that HE is the greatest blessing of all. *Behind a Frowning Providence*

June 2, 2015

One of the most difficult things to do when the road is rough or when the billows are passing over for us is to feel that God still loves us. It is the last thing we can accept. But we are not called to feel but to believe ... we are to measure God's love not by His providence, but by His promise. *Behind a Frowning Providence*

It is impossible to be submissive and patient [to God and His good will] if you stay your thoughts down among the second causes: 'O, the place! O, the time! O, if this had been, if this had not followed!' SAMUEL RUTHERFORD

When we cannot trace God's hand we can trust His heart. CHARLES SPURGEON

All things work together for the good for those who love God and are called according to His purpose. ROMANS 8:28

June 3, 2015

Increasingly convinced that gratitude is one of the most important aspects to every day. Even the hardest day can still be like drinking out of a fire hydrant of God's goodness. Whether it be the obvious blessings and beauties all around, more easily seen and felt. Or the deeper, sometimes more hidden, yet foundational truths of God and His promises.

Looking at it all with the eyes of thankfulness is like connecting the dots of God's provision and seeing a clearer picture of His presence and His sparkling good and merciful character.

Give thanks to the Lord for He is good. His steadfast love endures forever!

'Child,' said the voice, 'I am telling you your story, not hers. I tell no one any story but his own.'

'Who are* you?' asked Shasta.

'Myself,' said the Voice, very deep and low so that the earth shook: and again 'Myself,' loud and clear and gay: and then the third time 'Myself,' whispered so softly you could hardly hear it, and yet it seemed to come from all round you as if the leaves rustled with it.

Shasta was no longer afraid that the Voice belonged to something that would eat him, nor that it was the voice of a ghost. But a new and different sort of trembling came over him. Yet he felt glad too.

The mist was turning from black to gray and from gray to white. This must have begun to happen some time ago, but while he had been talking to the Thing he had not been noticing anything else. Now, the whiteness around him became a shining whiteness; his eyes began to blink. Somewhere ahead he could hear birds singing. He knew the night was over at last. He could see the mane and ears and head of his horse quite easily now. A golden light fell on them from the left. He thought it was the sun.

He turned and saw, pacing beside him, taller than the horse, a Lion. The horse did not seem to be afraid of it or else could not see it. It was from the Lion that the light came. No one ever say anything more terrible or beautiful … after one glance at the Lion's face he slipped out of the saddle and fell at its feet. He couldn't say anything but then he didn't want to say anything, and he knew he needn't say anything.

The High King above all kings stooped toward him. Its mane, and some strange and solemn perfume that hung about the mane, was all round him. It touched his forehead with its tongue. He lifted his face and their eyes met. Then instantly the pale brightness of the mist and the fiery brightness of the Lion rolled themselves together into a swirling glory and gathered themselves up and disappeared. He was alone with the horse on a grassy hillside under a blue sky. And there were birds singing.

C. S. Lewis, *The Horse and His Boy** (New York: Harper Trophy, 1998), 163-6.

June 3, 2015

Would you pray again for me? We are having a wonderful time, but for some reason I'm beginning to really struggle thinking about all those days in nuclear med department every day next week. Trying to just go back to savor the moment, not leap ahead. And if I do leap ahead, to force myself to paint a truer picture than my fears like to paint. One with every need provided for and grace for every step. Thanks so much for bearing with me through this!

> In times of anxiety, serenity;
> In times of hardship, courage;
> In times of uncertainty, patience;

And at all times, a quiet trust in your wisdom
and love; through Jesus Christ our Lord.

C.H. SPURGEON

June 6, 2015

> 'For My thoughts are not your thoughts, Nor are your
> ways My ways,' declares the LORD. 'For as the heavens are
> higher than the earth, So are My ways higher than your
> ways And My thoughts than your thoughts. For as the rain
> and the snow come down from heaven, And do not return
> there without watering the earth And making it bear and
> sprout, And furnishing seed to the sower and bread to
> the eater; So will My word be which goes forth from My
> mouth; It will not return to Me empty, …' ISAIAH 55:8-11

Surely every snag in our plans is really something unseen
but wonderful in His. His Word will not go out empty.
It will accomplish what He purposes. Just think of all the
promises He gives us! They are all dependable. We may take
them and set a particular (and usually straight) course for
them. Yet His much higher thoughts and ways take them
and shape them, making bends and mountains and valleys.
These do far more than we could have imagined with our
simple, flat, super-predictable super-highways of desires.

One day we will look back in joy on even the hardest,
most mysterious days and delight. It will be a panorama of
God's goodness and faithfulness. Oh, to borrow and live by
the joy of that day today! That is the joy of not seeing, but
faith. Praying to shine with it now! God is that good! He
can be trusted with everything!

ISAIAH 41:10

June 6, 2015

Back in DC! Want to thank you all for praying! It was amazing how God kindly, abundantly, powerfully heard and answered your prayers. We had what must be the nicest time away in two years. It was obvious that it was something given especially as a result of all the prayers. Had very few freak outs about what is ahead this week. And even the big one that I did have, after I asked you to pray, within minutes it subsided and left ... This is Even more remarkable when looked at in contrast with how hard I ineffectively fought it on my own for a few hours before asking you to pray. He loves to remind us that He is with us and is the Great One who does all things well. That, too, was a good reminder for what's ahead and His ability to carry me through – just have to ask.

June 7, 2015

> Therefore, since we are surrounded by so great
> a cloud of witnesses, let us also lay aside every
> weight, and sin which clings so closely, and let us
> run with endurance the race that is set before us,
> looking to Jesus, the author and perfecter of our
> faith. HEBREWS 12:1-2

The race set out for us! Makes me think of the track and field events from school days. Multiple events taking place at the same time. You never did all of the events, just the one or few that your coach chose for you, according to what your skills were and which would be best to help your team win at the meet.

This is us! We have an event, a race set out for us. Our Coach has chosen it for us. He's trained us for it. He hadn't signed us up for the mile when we really should be doing the fifty yard dash. He knows what He's doing. Long distance it is, because endurance He provides!

Author of our faith … Perfecter of our faith … The one who gives us our beginning and carries us through to the finish line. The great Coach of the biggest group of Couch to 10k-ers you ever did see! So glad to not have to try to run alone. His grace has been abundantly sufficient for so many before us and around us! It will be abundantly sufficient for us, too!

> The world says, 'Perform.' Jesus says, 'Rest.'
> TIM KELLER, @timkellernyc

June 7, 2015

Just in case anyone is curious … Here's what Week 1 of radiation appreciation month looks like. ☺

Mon. 9 a.m. prep injection 1 and blood work.

Tues. 9 a.m. prep injection 2.

Wed. 9 a.m. radioactive iodine small dose first three hours of scans and blood work (have to fast most of the day … NOT part of my skill set.

Thurs. 9 a.m. blood work and short scan.

Fri. 9 a.m. blood and longest day of scans.

Sat. 9 a.m. blood and short scan.

Mon. 9 a.m. blood and short scan

From all of this data, they will then make their best calculation of max dose of radiation to give me that won't permanently damage my bone marrow and lungs. (The process for giving me that big dose will start up on Mon June 22).

Please pray for good judgement about the dose and for me to have good veins. I typically have very fussy veins. Never had so much blood drawn so frequently. And pray that I will be an encouragement to the staff in nuclear medicine that I've already gotten to know from other treatment. Would love to commend the great God to whom I belong. And lastly, that I'd rest into Him with all of this. He's good but it's still ugh business to go through. Can't do it alone!

Thanks for praying!

June 8, 2015

> May the God of hope fill you with all joy and peace as
> you trust in him, that you may overflow with joy through
> the power of the Holy Spirit. ROMANS 15:13

June 8, 2015

Day 1 down. Sick a lot today from injection and a lot of arm pain from hitting a nerve in the blood draw … But much better now! Glad for only an injection tomorrow. Veins get the day off. Delightful evening playing maybe the most random game ever … Killer Bunnies! Thanks for praying!

June 10, 2015

Thanks so much for praying! Made it through the long fast and the scan and blood work! Back into isolation through Sun.

For God alone, O my soul, wait in silence,
 for my hope is from him.

He only is my rock and my salvation,
 my fortress; I shall not be shaken.
On God rests my salvation and my glory;
 my mighty rock, my refuge is God.

PSALM 62:5-7

God is most glorified in us when we are most
satisfied in Him.
 JOHN PIPER, www.christianquotes.info

June 10, 2015
Ugh So sick!

June 11, 2015
Wow! Terribly sick all night! Hoping for some relief today
as this radiation works its way out. Thanks for your prayers!
Just got to get to the hospital and back for a short scan and
will consider it a productive day!

June 11, 2015
Home! Thank you for praying! Hope to do lots of resting!
Tomorrow will be a long day of various scans and quite a bit
more blood. But at least no fasting! Yay! Go food! They hit
a nerve again today and are having far more trouble getting
blood than ever in me. I still have Fri, Sat, and Mon to go
and they are already giving up on arm veins. Those would
be wonderful things to pray for for tomorrow if you think
of it! Thanks for walking with me in this!

June 12, 2015

Just finished my long day of scans and spoke to the doctor. They still see activity in the neck and this is the confirmation they needed regarding the big radiation dose coming up on June 25. Now I certainly would not have minded having a clear scan today and opting for a trip to the Bahamas instead of a hospital room later this month, but I'm grateful for this confirmation that this is the path I need to go on.

Blood work continues to be very difficult. They can only use very small veins now and it took fifteen minutes and two technicians working together to get three small tubes of blood today. Please pray for God to help me and my veins through two more days of blood draws. Thanks for caring!

> But you, O Lord, are a shield about me,
>   my glory, and the lifter of my head.
>
> Psalm 3:3

June 13, 2015

The veins were very, very happy and eager to share this morning. Remarkably different! Thanks for praying!

June 4, 2015

> They couldn't read, but they had heard the
> stories so many times that they could tell it by
> the pictures. *The Bent Twig*

> Not a thing had happened the way she had planned
> it. No, not a single thing, but it seemed she had
> never been so happy in all her life.
>
> *Understood Betsy*

Two quotes from children's books I've read lately. Both of them struck me as remarkably clear bells of truth that I've been appreciating as of late. That life always comes with so many unexpected twists and turns. So many unknowns. So much of what we could never plan, would never plan. And yet, with the Lord, it is the same story of redemption over and over and over.

I do not have 'eyes' to read the whole story of my life of which the Lord says every day is already written in His book. But have I not 'heard' the story so many times in what He has done in those who have gone before me and who live along side me and those from long ago in God's Word? Can't I tell from those life pictures much of my story? It will end well.

Oh sure, there will be many struggles. Oh sure, I will fail and there will be fear and pain. There will even be death, eventually. Ah, but through all of this, those who wait upon the Lord will not faint. Those who trust in Him will never be put to shame. With Him there is redemption. And because of redemption, there is Resurrection. Worthless things made precious, Dead things raised with power to life. Both of these things. Both on a daily basis and as the final trajectory of my life. There is weighty hope that sparkles on the unknown path ahead in faint glimmers all around like morning dew, and rises all the way up to heaven in a trail that never ends.

God is that good. He is that right. He is that trustworthy. The lives of those who put their lives in His hands are just another chance for Him to re-tell His story in us. They are His answer to the cry, 'Daddy, tell me the story again.' And He does. Over and over in our lives.

Yes … Nothing turned out as she planned. Not, a single thing, but it seemed that she had never been so happy in all her life.

Better is one day in His courts than a thousand elsewhere.

June 15, 2015
Scared Today

June 15, 2015

Well I can't believe my ears!!! My doctor just called me. Total reversal of everything that the nuclear med and endocrinology team were saying even Friday. I guess they got my blood work back today and said absolutely everything was undetectable! Even my antibody levels, even my cancer markers everything. My levels have never looked anything like this! There is still a nodule that is growing and that still shows up. But bc all the other levels have been completely knocked out, they will just watch it not treat it!

So no more big radiation. No need at this time! Appointment for June 25th is cancelled. Just another day. Wow! God has been kind to bear me through this. You have been kind to pray. He would be faithful and use it for good if I had to go through it … But I am so so so happy and grateful that at least for now, this trial is DONE!

And I'm so going to go eat something with eggs and dairy and iodized salt and lots and lots of MEAT!!!!!! (So glad to be off this crazy low iodine diet!)

Praise the Lord for this sweet sweet gift to me today!

And he awoke and rebuked the wind and said to the sea, 'Peace! Be still!' And the wind ceased, and there was a great calm. MARK 4:39

June 16, 2015

I am overwhelmed with all your kind words! So many of you have prayed and cared! Wow! Thank you!

It's been a weird day of re-orienting myself to life without this big THING over me, under me, around me. I'm grateful and completely shocked that He has chosen to remove this from me (at least for now.) Not because of any doubt that He could take it away, but because it has so obviously borne such necessary fruit in me and I can see so much more work needed. He was good and right to give this to me.

Sounds strange probably, but I'm almost scared for Him to take it away. Afraid I will forget what I've learned. I don't want to go back. I want to keep yearning to be always closer to Him. I want to grow. He's shown me the the way of fellowship with Him is reliance upon Him. In strong-willed humans like me, this seems to comes most assuredly by being made weak first. I love how Paul Tripp says he starts each day praying to God, 'I am weak, needy and rebellious and need grace for this day.' He is right! May I never forget it! I have come to love watching God provide riches on even the most penniless days. I am still a pauper now, just not one with active cancer with seemingly constant in-your-face repercussions. Oh to keep begging! To live each day His way and watching for His work!

And maybe at least I will receive any hard yoke that comes next – whenever or whatever that is – with less trepidation because He has led me through a little bit of the valley of the shadow of death and has done so with wisdom, mercy, goodness and compassion. And I'm sure this experience is no exception with the Lord, the Good Shepherd of His people.

Oh taste and see that the Lord is good! PSALM 34

> I realized that the deepest spiritual lessons are not learned by His letting us have our way in the end, but by His making us wait, bearing with us in love and patience until we are able to honestly to pray what He taught His disciples to pray: Thy will be done.
>
> ELIZABETH ELLIOT *Passion and Purity:*
> *Learning to bring your life under Christ's control.*

June 18, 2015

> Let him who walks in darkness and has no light, trust in the name of the Lord and rely on his God. ISAIAH 50:10

God's name, that is, His character is steadfast. We may want to react like roly-poly bugs that roll up in fear at the sound of the giant footsteps of trouble and don't know what to do but try to protect ourselves and hide. We may have NO LIGHT. Our understanding of what we are going through may be 'dark' and everything be terrifying. But God's character means that He is always enough. We do not have to depend only on ourselves to get us through our troubles and keep us safe. God promises to take care of those who cry out and put their trust in Him... And He will never break His promises. The darkness is as light to Him. He knows every foe and is stronger than them all. Everything fits perfectly within His plans. We can trust and rest in Him! The curve of the palm of His hand in which we rest is the only protective shell we need. So be of good cheer fellow roly-polies!

And just in case you don't know what a roly-poly is ... https://en.m.wikipedia.org/wiki/Armadillidiidae

They are my favorite bug next to the firefly ... OK and ladybugs.

June 23, 2015

> I will run in the way of your commandments when
> you enlarge my heart! PSALM 119:32

God Himself gives us greater obedience to Him by Himself growing our heart's affections. Even when we don't want to obey, but only WANT to want to obey, He meets us there and provides. There is no heart too far away that He cannot change. We can ask Him to soften the unruliness of our heart right where it is. And by changing our heart, He changes our whole course. What a gracious, powerful God there is in heaven! Standing ready! What are we waiting for?!

> Come, ye sinners, poor and needy,
> Weak and wounded, sick and sore;
> Jesus ready stands to save you,
> Full of pity, love and power.
>
> REFRAIN:
> *I will arise and go to Jesus,*
> *He will embrace me in His arms;*
> *In the arms of my dear Savior,*
> *O there are ten thousand charms.*
> *Come, ye thirsty, come, and welcome,*

God's free bounty glorify;
True belief and true repentance,
Every grace that brings you nigh.

REFRAIN:

Come, ye weary, heavy laden,
Lost and ruined by the fall;
If you tarry till you're better,
You will never come at all.

REFRAIN:

JOSEPH HART

June 25, 2015

> I will bless the Lord at all times. His praise will continually be on my mouth. PSALM 34:1

I should have been at the hospital getting a huge dose of radiation right now. Instead … I am going up to the mountains. Thank you, Lord! Whether it be a permanent healing or just a respite, I am grateful for this particularly unexpected gift.

June 25, 2015

> Even to your old age I am he, and to gray hairs I will carry you. I have made, and I will bear; I will carry and will save. ISAIAH 46:4

This sounds like the promise a husband or wife might make to their dearly loved spouse. And sweet certainly is such a promise when made! And how true, up to our finite limits.

But finite we are, and so, unreliable are even our best kept promises. Our best promises and hopes get battered by the insecurities of this broken world and our broken selves within it.

But the wonderful thing about this promise is that it isn't the promise of a husband or wife to their spouse. This is a promise of the Lord to His people. The God who says He betrothes us to Himself forever (Hosea 2:19). And when this God makes a promise, we can count on it!

He has omnipotence to back it up. He has every one of our days planned and firmly held in His always capable hands. His love is what shapes and sets in place every event of our life. He promises to carry us all the way through and so He will! This is a 100 per cent sure thing. We can rest in His arms no matter what the alarms!

June 28, 2015

> There is no fear in love, but perfect love casts out fear. For fear has to do with punishment, and whoever fears has not been perfected in love. We love because he first loved us. I JOHN 4:18-19

Sometimes I feel chided when I read these verses. If I only had more love, I would fear less. If I only truly believed, deeply, that my punishment has been ended in Christ, by what He's done for me on the cross. If only I could better grasp that everything that God does is coming to me out of love, then I would be free from fear. God is certainly deserving of my perfect love because He is perfect, as is His love for me.

These things are most certainly true, but still, this side of heaven, I think I'm going to struggle with fear, with not having as much trust in God as I could, and certainly as I should.

But if I let verses like these batter me, instead of comfort me, then I think I'm missing the point. The point is how great God's love is. How powerful it is to drive out my fear. He will persevere in His love. He will have His way with me. I am being perfected by Him. He is the action and I WILL be the reaction, praise God! And while I don't know how much of this will be achieved this side of heaven, or how much will have to wait until I am in His presence, and all is changed and seen for what it really was and is. But either way, God's love will drive out my fear. That is nothing but fantastic news!

And I am grateful that while my vision maybe blurry and dim, and I don't see things as I should, at least He's given me some sight. And even that little bit of sight, excites me about what more of Him and His love and basking in it there is ahead. He is the one who first loved me. Surely that is the best news, the greatest reason to hope that we can ever have or need! He is the author and finisher of our faith. That is what counts most of all.

July 1, 2015

> He who goes out weeping, bearing the seed for
> sowing, shall come home with shouts of joy, bringing
> his sheaves with him. PSALM 126:6

Don't God's promises give wonderful things to those who trust in Him? Not only are there the things He gives us and we enjoy that are easy seen as blessings. But also, in our sorrows and trials, He so orders things that we hold in our hands the seeds of future fruit. Watered by our tears, sprouting by His work in our hearts, He fills our arms with good things that bring us joy.

How good the Lord is to us! Even on our most difficult days we can know that He has placed seeds in our hand to sow. It is never the final word. Sorrow always means a work in progress, never the end, for those who love God. Complete, lasting joy is always our destination. And knowing that, we can borrow on that future, complete joy and live in it today.

July 6, 2015

> Have I been a wilderness to Israel, or a land of
> thick darkness? Why then do my people say,
> 'We will come to you no more'?
>
> Can a virgin forget her ornaments, or a bride
> her attire? Yet my people have forgotten me days
> without number ... How well you direct your
> course to seek love! ... How much you go about,
> changing your way!
> From JEREMIAH 2

These verses remind me to look to the loves of my heart today. They chart my course. They need to be examined and usually redirected back to the Lord's ways and plans.

He is our good husband. He is the one who truly satisfies. He is always worth waiting for. But my heart loves to be satisfied now. Every day I am like Israel of old. I tempted to direct my own course and fill my many heart-hungers in my own way, in my own time, with things that provide only short-term satisfaction. Oh, my wonderful God, who knows best, does best and loves best! Help me to always choose to set down the quick-fix before me and wait upon You and Your perfect, fully-satisfying plans and ways!

July 8, 2015

Dwelling today upon some of the great rescues of the Bible: The slaves from the land of Egypt: the parting of the Red Sea, the manna and quail in the wilderness, the Ark of the covenant and the Israelites crossing the Jordan River on dry ground at flood stage, the flattening of the Assyrian army outside of Jerusalem; and Lazarus raised from the dead to name a few.

One thing is clear: for God's people, dire circumstances are merely the stage for a greater show of God's faithfulness.

What wonderful news is this to hold on to, no matter what comes our way today! He always has a plan. He always makes a way. He always will provide. He will always show Himself to be more than we could ever need or imagine.

Our journey here may be filled with unknowns from our perspective, but there is always a reason for joy and hope and even rest. He who loves us Is so good and so great. I am so grateful to be His!

July 8, 2015

I am so grateful that in this world there is no risk for God's people. There is only the appearance of risk. And even that appearance of risk is but a tool of our sweet Fatger to grow our trust in Him.

He has every single one of our days measured out. There will always be everything we need. He had laid up in store everything He knew we would need – way in advance. That's one of the workings out of His planning our every day in advance. And can not you look back and see only His faithfulness?

I'm not saying that everything has been easy or fun. But has He not used them all for our good and His glory. Isn't that wonderful!

Psalm 91

1. Those who live in the shelter of the Most High will find rest in the shadow of the Almighty.

2. This I declare about the Lord:
   He alone is my refuge, my place of safety; He is my God, and I trust Him.

3. For He will rescue you from every trap and protect you from deadly disease.

4. He will cover you with His feathers. He will shelter you with His wings. His faithful promises are your armor and protection.

5. Do not be afraid of the terrors of the night, nor the arrow that flies in the day.

6. Do not dread the disease that stalks in darkness, nor the disaster that strikes at midday.

7. Though a thousand fall at your side, though ten thousand are dying around you, these evils will not touch you.

8. Just open your eyes, and see how the wicked are punished.

9. If you make the Lord your refuge, if you make the Most High your shelter,

10. No evil will conquer you; no plague will come near your home.

11. For He will order his angels to protect you wherever you go.

12. They will hold you up with their hands so you won't even hurt your foot on a stone.

13. You will trample upon lions and cobras; you will crush fierce lions and serpents under your feet!

14. The Lord says, 'I will rescue those who love me. I will protect those who trust in my name.

15. When they call on me, I will answer; I will be with them in trouble. I will rescue and honor them.

16. I will reward them with a long life and give them my salvation.'

July 8, 2015

Over and over God calls me to release when I so dearly want to cling. Release my understanding, release my control, release forms of security. So that at last, I will cling to Him. And in Him find far more than I ever released in the first place.

July 8, 2015

> For I know the plans I have for you, declares the
> Lord, plans for welfare and not for evil, to give you a
> future and a hope. JEREMIAH 29:11

Why is it that most days it seems that I am calling a rematch of my wits versus the Lord's? He says, 'Trust me!' Make what you know of Me the lens through which you make sense of what you see or feel or think!

He knows the plans He has for me even when I do not. Believe, my heart! Be thankful! Trust! Wait!

16. But I will sing of your strength; I will sing aloud of your steadfast love in the morning. For you have been to me a fortress and a refuge in the day of my distress. 17. O my Strength, I will sing praises to you, for you, O God, are my fortress, the God who shows me steadfast love. Psalm 59

July 13, 2015

To be wise, first you need to be rescued from you. You need to be given a new heart, one that is needy, humble, seeking, and ready to get from above what you can't find on this earth.

Paul David Tripp *New Morning Mercies*

July 13, 2015

Paul David Tripp continues to knock it out of the park for me. Just started his book called *Whiter than Snow* which is a series of meditations based on Psalm 51.

Here's an excerpt from chapter 1:

It was one of those moments you want to take back. It was one of those times when you go where your desires and emotions are leading you. It was one of those situations when you know you should stop or walk away but feel you can't. And it was one of those moments when afterwards you are confronted with the sin that still lives inside of you. Yes it was one of those moments.

It wasn't a big deal in one way ... But maybe that's the point. ... You see, you and I don't live in a series of big, dramatic moments. We don't career from big decision to big decision. We all live in an endless series of little moments. The character of a life isn't set in ten big moments. The character of a life is set in 10,000 little moments of every day life. It's the themes of struggles that emerge from those little moments that reveal what's really going on in our hearts.

PAUL TRIP, *Whiter Than Snow*/PSALM 51

That's just a taste from the beginning of a very good book. Thank you again, Paul Tripp! God has used you mightily in my soul!

I will give thanks to the Lord with my whole heart; I will recount all of your wonderful deeds. I will be glad and exult in you; I will sing praise to your name, O Most High. PSALM 9:1-2 ESV

July 16, 2015

So from now on we regard no one from a worldly point of view. 2 CORINTHIANS 5:16

All things work together for those who love God and are called according to His purpose. ROMANS 8:28

Nothing can separate us from God's love in Christ. ROMANS 8:39

Your eyes saw my unformed body; all the days ordained for me were written in your book before one of them came to be. PSALM 139:16

For I know the plans I have for you ... plans for welfare, not for evil, to give you a future and a hope ... . JEREMIAH 29:11

This may or may not be a good day, according to my plans. But it most certainly will be a good day according to God's plans and His plans for me ... And even His plans going forward through me. Wow!

Trying to make of a habit of asking God to keep this foremost in my perspective, as the day unfolds. To not view or respond to anyone or anything from that two-dimensional 'worldly perspective.'

Want to be alert. Standing ready to respond, to appreciate, to make the most of, what God planned for this day of His making. His Kingdom come! His will be done! There always is a plan with God and His people. It's not a good plan ... It's the best plan.

July 16, 2015
Would you please pray for the Lord of all creation to cause the wind to calm down up here at Wintergreen? It's a long story ... but it would be miraculously wonderful for it to die down and stay away today and tomorrow!

July 16, 2015
Thanks for praying! The wind died down remarkably just in time. And the Lord showed once more to the guys working up here that it is He who calms the wind! Grateful for the testimony. We've been waiting weeks for the right conditions to stain. Very difficult to get up here on this mountain. Need two more days of this. Back on my knees! Nothing from a worldly perspective!

July 17, 2015
> We all tend to be way too trusting of our view of ourselves. We do this because we do not take seriously what the Bible says about the dynamic of spiritual

blindness. If sin is deceitful and it is, if sin blinds and it does, then as long as sin still works inside of me, there will be patches of spiritual blindness. I simply do not see myself with the accuracy that I think I do … . Sin causes me to be all too convinced of my righteousness and all too focused on your sin.

Paul David Tripp *New Morning Mercies*

A wonderful reminder of why we shouldn't be lone cowboy Christians. A wonderful reminder of why we need to read God's Word each day.

To not have others to speak into your life, to not have God's word to speak into your life, is like choosing to be blind, when you could see, if you would just put on your glasses. Thank you, Lord, for your word! Thank you, for your church!

July 18, 2015

Wonderful night of thanksgiving for so many good gifts from this past year. And the best part is how many have come in the form of understanding God more and drawing closer to Him. He is gentle, He is powerful, He is a fountain of grace, He is the great planner and weaver, He is persistent, He is the provider, He is the master of the storms, He is better than life.

July 19, 2015

The Bible never denies reality. The Bible never plays it safe. The Bible never tricks you into thinking that things are better than they are. The Bible is straightforward and honest but not void of hope. While it is very candid about the hardships of life in

this broken world, the Bible is also gloriously hopeful.
The honesty does not crush the hope, but neither
does the hope negate the honesty.

God's grace calls you to suffer and it calls you to wait,
but it never calls you to stand in your own strength or to
stand alone.

Grace doesn't help you just to do different things but
to become a totally different person by changing you at
the level of your heart.

New Morning Mercies, PAUL DAVID TRIPP

And God is able to make all grace abound to you, so
that in all things at all times, having all you need, you
will abound in every good work. As it is written: 'He has
scattered abroad his gifts to the poor; his righteousness
endures forever.' 2 CORINTHIANS 9:8, 9

I am the vine; you are the branches. If you remain in me
and I in you, you will bear much fruit; apart from me
you can do nothing. JOHN 15:5

We cannot help but look ahead in fear at what might lie
ahead, if we look to our own supply.
WE ARE HOPELESSLY POOR!
But we can confidently face whatever lies ahead, when
we look at His supply. By independence, we can do nothing.
By dependence, we can do it all.
HE IS FABULOUSLY RICH!

O Lord, help us to know and to live by both of
these truths!
So sing for joy, dear afflicted one,
The battle's fierce, but the victory's won,

God shall supply all that you need,
For as your days,
Your strength shall be.

July 21, 2015

I thought I knew better. I thought I knew exactly what was coming next. I had written the next chapter of my story. But I had forgotten that someone else was the author … Your story isn't an autobiography either. Your story is a biography of wisdom and grace written by another. Every turn He writes into your story is right. Every twist of the plot is for the best. Every new character and unexpected event is a tool of His grace. Each new chapter advances His purpose.

Whoever is wise, let him understand these things; whoever is discerning, let him know them; for the ways of the Lord are right. HOSEA 14:9

It is almost a gross understatement to say that God's ways are better. How could they not be? He is infinite in wisdom and grace!

PAUL TRIPP *New Morning Mercies*

Me:

I look back and see that God always knew best and did best.

I look around me today and sometimes see that He knows best and is doing best.

I look forward to the future and get unhinged with concern that He won't know best or do best.

Be still, my soul, and rest, even be excited, in God! While my hindsight is not even close to 20-20, God's oversight of today, and His foresight of tomorrow, as well as His hindsight of yesterday, are all perfect!

July 21, 2015

Day fourteen of this lesson called 'Ask Me for what seems impossible.' Should have been rain yet again today, but God kept it at bay, allowing a bit more of the outdoor work to get done. So hoping to be finished this week after months and months of work. Rain clouds, rain clouds, rain clouds, but very little rain! Grateful!

God would be just as good to let it rain, if that would be better for what He knows is best. But, He has made this daily exercise of me asking and depending on Him to hold back the skies as a daily reminder to pray for more than I can imagine in the lives of many. Live by faith, not by sight! Been a wonderful lesson and time of praying big things.

July 22, 2015

> 'For I know the plans I have for you,' declares the
> Lord, 'plans to prosper you and not to harm you,
> plans to give you hope and a future. Then you will
> call upon me and come and pray to me, and I will
> listen to you. You will seek me and find me when you
> seek me with all your heart. I will be found by you,'
> declares the LORD. JEREMIAH 29:11-14

I am borrowing off of this promise the LORD, long ago, made to the people of Israel. It was given to them while they were in captivity in Babylon. It seems like it was a double captivity. Captivity physically, as they were the slaves of the Babylonians and away from their homeland. But just as much, it was the captivity of their hearts. That's what the Lord was disciplining in the first place, when they would not listen to His warnings to turn back to Him, but kept on worshipping idols and depending on the power of the countries around them rather than on Him.

For me too, there are strong temptations each day to look for security, prosperity, and control in things or people other than the Lord.

And like the Israelites, I need to address the heart issue behind my life issues. To seek to enjoy, and perhaps most of all, employ the many good gifts that the Lord has placed within my reach for His glory, without falling into the trap of trusting in them for security.

How good He was to Israel when He disciplined them! How good He is to us when He disciplines us and shows us where our allegiances lie.

His prosperity is best. His plans are best. And in Him is truly hope and all the future we could need or want. Far better than anything we can work up ourselves.

O, LORD, show me what it means to seek You with all my heart and help me to do that. Help me to be found by You … And increasingly so! My heart, my life, my all for You and whatever You desire!

July 28, 2015

God is so big and so able! I have been overwhelmed lately with the magnificent way that He weaves everything together, works things out, plans things in advance, and shows up right on time.

What an amazing privilege it is to be His daughter and to be given eyes to see what must really be just the glimmers of His plans, His wisdom and love.

And what security there is to run to His arms, to offer up my requests. To not even have to have a clue as to how He will take care of everything … and yet rest, knowing that He can and He will. Yes! Rest!

> Come to me, all who labor and are heavy laden, and I will give you rest. Take my yoke upon you, and learn from me, for I am gentle and lowly in heart, and you will find rest for your souls. For my yoke is easy, and my burden is light. MATTHEW 11:28-30

He gives the weary a yoke to wear. They will have to set aside doing things their own way, in their own time. But in doing so, He gives them rest from labor – that toil that seems to go nowhere and leads to nothing. That independence we love that is really far more like a gerbil wheel than it is the yellow brick road we hoped it would be.

Did you notice that these words were recorded in Matthew's gospel? He was a tax collector living the high life funded by the riches he extorted from others. This made him an outcast from synagogue and Temple. No access to God under the Law. But he left his highway post and the riches behind to follow Jesus. He knew all about the heavy burden of that independent life that looks so good and free. He found something … Someone … better.

He gives the weary a yoke to wear, but it is not the law, as some might think. It is not a long list of dreary, dry dos and don'ts. It is not scoring up good deeds. It is grace. He, Himself, has borne the labor of keeping all the law. He has fulfilled it and made the final sacrifice for us. He did what we could never do. The yoke of labor is retired for us.

His yoke is a yoke of rest, of grace. It is restful because He knows what we can bear. We could never bear all the works of the law. Only His back could and did. And so He is able to give us only what we can bear. His gentleness weighs it out and places it on our back.

And it is restful because there is a steady purpose in it. There is always a guaranteed fruitfulness. Always fulfilling His plans. Always headed towards home.

And it is restful because it is always and only by grace. That is, He always will give us what we need to walk every step, and He will give it to us step by step… by Holy Spirit living in our hearts…comforting, strengthening, guiding, and even transforming us.

A new yoke for those He calls His new creations. Bought through the new covenant in Jesus' blood and brought through His Spirit … New life. Oh how beautiful! Oh how wonderful!

Come, weary! Set down your labor! Take up His yoke. Find rest in Him! It's the only place it can be found!

July 31, 2015

Two quotes from Jeremiah 27:

> With my great power and outstretched arm I made the earth and its people and the animals that are on it, and I give it to anyone I please.

> For this is what the Lord Almighty says about the pillars, the sea, the movable stands and the other furnishings (all objects from the temple) that are left in the city … 'They will be taken to Babylon and

there they will remain until the day I come for them,'
declares the Lord. 'Then I will bring them back and
restore them (the people) to this place.'

How mighty is the Lord! He does whatever pleases Him.
These two verses have to do with how the Lord would use
the great super power of Babylon for His good purposes
for His people. He would be behind these great events of
history, moving even great armies and kings to fit His plans.

I'm sure Nebuchadnezzar believed he was gorging himself on the riches of the Temple when he took all these
beautiful things back to Babylon after destroying Jerusalem.
But the Lord was only using him as a storage unit for these
things as well as a time-out space for His rebellious people.
In His perfect timing they would be restored to their place.
How very different the Lord's perspective from ours!

He is not the great mover behind every movement? His
good plans will always take place! He is always at work.
This is reason always for faith and for hope. This is reason
to pray! Nothing is outside His realm of influence ...
Whether it be the mess in the world around us or the mess
in the world inside us!

August 3, 2015

> Now it is God who makes both us and you stand firm
> in Christ. He anointed us, set his seal of ownership
> on us, and put his Spirit in our hearts as a deposit,
> guaranteeing what is to come. 2 CORINTHIANS 1:21-22

The Holy Spirit in our hearts is like the engagement ring
that our wonderful bridegroom-to-be has given us. Just

225

think. Now we enjoy such gifts from Him: His wisdom. His comfort. His power. His boldness. His help. His fruit in our lives that gives us joy, love, self-control, patience, kindness, goodness, and peace.

Yet these are but a tiny taste of the life ahead with Him. Life ahead here, because He delights to give more of His Spirit to those who ask. And life ahead in heaven, because there we will have the fullness of our relationship with Him in bloom. The love letters of our long-distance engagement will cease. And the face to face forever fellowship will begin and never end.

August 3, 2015
Love is a giving. A self-forgetfulness. It isn't looking to protect itself, but it is busy seeking after the good of the one loved.

Love is a receiving, too, as we reveal ourselves honestly to each other. A trust that opens oneself up in vulnerability. That says, 'What I have, I will show you and give to you. I will let you in so close and tie my life to yours so intimately that I am willing to leave myself in a position for you to even be able to hurt me.'

Love is wonderful, but it is scary, too, especially when it is between humans. We are often clumsy mis-handlers of the love we give and receive.

But not so God. He is always trustworthy. His love is pure and perfect. We might not always understand His love when certain things happen. I guess that's where the scariness of His love can come in for us – that we can't always understand and therefore sometimes are tempted to doubt it.

But over and over He shows His love to be perfect. 'Trust me! Trust me!' His faithfulness encourages us. 'Give me your heart, your life. Find your life in Me! Come, belong to Me.'

Isn't it amazing that the God of the universe desires to show us love and for us to love Him! In Him is the most exquisite of loves. What a privilege!

August 8, 2015
Thinking about dependence today.

Dependence upon someone else can be tinged with different hues … .

FEAR … If we think about being dependent upon someone who does not want us to depend upon them or who is unreliable

OUT OF CONTROL … . Related to fear, we must rely upon someone else and that someone else may have different ideas sbout what we need or when we need it. Or, we doubt their desire or power to make sure we have what we need.

BUT ALSO …

REST AND PEACE … When we are assured that the one we are dependent on has the wisdom, the power, the desire and commitment to take care of us.

Most people have someone who reflects at least bits of this side of committed care in their life. How very grateful I am for the people who do that in mine.

But how much more grateful am I for the God who is the Sun and the Source of the care of these dear people. They may come and go. Their love may ebb and flow. But He never will leave or forsake. His love endures and provides forever.

Surely child-like faith comes the closer we move to our Heavenly Father, in dependence! What a picture of Himself He had left us in His Son He did not spare in order to graft us into His family! How dependable He is to take care of us! How He delights for us to snuggle up next to Him and lean into His everlasting arms!

He created us for dependency. It is no burden to Him. It is the highway of the fellowship of His presence. If we want to know God we will seek dependence upon Him.

Dependence looks like prayer – worship of Him, confessing our sins, thanking Him, and asking Him for what we need. It looks like God's Word – knowing it, reading it, living off of it. Dependence looks at the 'seen' with the lens of the 'unseen' to filter the impossible out of the most impossible situation.

I long to live this way! I long to know more of the joyful, restful, delightful fellowship side of dependence! By God's gracious help, may it be so!

August 13, 2015

> Most of our hopes disappoint us. We all do it. We place our hope in things in this fallen world that simply can't deliver. Your spouse can't make you happy. Your job won't make you content. Your possessions can't satisfy your heart. Your physical health won't give you inner peace. Your friends can't give you meaning and purpose. When our hopes disappoint us, it is a sign that we've put our hopes in the wrong things.

There are only two places to look for hope. The theology of hope is quite simple. There are only two places to put your hope. You rest the hope of your life in the hands of the Creator or you look to the creation for hope.

Hope in God is sure hope. When you hope in the Lord, you not only hope in the One who created and controls the universe, but also in One who is glorious in grace and abounding in love. Now, that's hope that is well placed and will never disappoint.

Yep. Paul Tripp again!

I notice that what I treasure, I fear and I hope at first seem to be quite different things, but really, the closer I look, they are really all drinking the same kool-aid. Oh, Lord, create in me a pure heart!

What do I lose when I have a praying life? Control. Independence. What do I gain? Friendship with God. A quiet heart. The living work of God in the hearts of those I love. The ability to roll back the tide of evil. Essentially, I lose my kingdom and get his. I move from being an independent player to a dependent lover. I move from being an orphan to a child of God.

PAUL E. MILLER *A Praying Life*

There will be moments when you will feel unprepared for what is on your plate. In these moments, look up and remember that above it all there is a throne, and on it sits a God of unimaginable majesty, ruling all for His glory and for your good.

PAUL TRIPP *New Morning Mercies*

August 15, 2015

> … Your comforts bring me joy … Psalm 94:19

God has filled His Word with the promise of so much comfort! Not necessarily ease, but definitely comfort.

And just like a box of the old-fashioned wind-up toy soldiers, I'm going to take them out one by one today, wind them up and set them to marching around me. His promises never run out, but my focus does. I'm in constant need of re-winding and reminding.

August 23, 2015

The lessons in dependence upon God continue for me. Many times for me, when the extent of my inability to depend upon myself or circumstances or others becomes more obvious, my response is fear. Dependence puts the welfare of my life in someone else's court … . And I don't want it to be there. I guess that's because deep down I still equate self-preservation with self-rule … self-responsibility.

Responsibility is the other side of dependence. If someone is dependent, then someone else is responsible. Who that is and what they are like makes all the difference. Dependence would be a truly scary thing if there were a malevolent person given the job of being responsible for me. It would even be a pretty scary thing if the person had good intentions but was either inept or ill-equipped to be responsible for me. The sad truth is that I am that person who is inept and ill-equipped to be responsible for myself in the big ways I try to be. None of us are cut out to live independently and be self-responsible without God. Nope.

God made us and God sustains us. We are created for His care.

There will be no full rest or peace without that relationship of my dependence and His responsibility. But what rest there can be when we accept this and live here!

Just think: the best Person who has ever been and ever will be has chosen to be responsible for my well-being. No one cares more than God. No one knows better than God. No one has done more to preserve me than God. No one has given me more promises and fulfilled them than God. No one has ever wanted to be responsible for me more than Him. He has adopted me as His child through Christ. Forever His. Forever safe. Forever provided for. Forever loved.

How wonderful! How undeserved! How I want to live deeper in the truth of His responsibility for me!

August 24, 2015

> Steadfast love surrounds the one who trusts
> in the Lord, be glad in the Lord and rejoice,
> O righteous. PSALM 32:10

Steadfast … . Not going anywhere, any time. Always on task, always committed, always available, always the same motive.

What motive? What agenda? LOVE! Perfect love. Perfectly wise and pure.

What does it do? SURROUND the one who trusts in The Lord. Protecting completely. Not missing a single thing that comes towards us from the front or even behind. He sees all. Knows all. Takes care of all. We may be easily blind-sided, but never Him!

And He either keeps things from us or employs them all for His loving purposes in our life. Our good. His glory.

What a wonderful God we have! Be still, my soul! Find your rest in God! Underneath you, all around you, are the Everlasting Arms.

August 26, 2015

> The steadfast love of the Lord never ceases, his mercies never come to an end; they are new every morning; great is your faithfulness. The Lord is my portion, says my soul, therefore I will hope in him. LAMENTATIONS 3:22-24

I am very familiar with these verses. The shocker came when I actually read all of Lamentations 3 and put them in context. If you've not done this lately, you may be amazed, too. Listen to this: 'I am the man who has seen affliction under the rod of his wrath; he has driven and brought me into darkness without any light; Surely against me he turns his hand again and again the whole day long. He has made my flesh and my skin waste away; he's broken my bone; he has beseiged and enveloped me with bitterness and tribulation; he had made me dwell in darkness like the dead of long ago.' ... And so it continues for an additional seventeen verses.

This is a man under severe affliction. Everywhere he turns is difficulty. It is a hurricane force storm that consumes and seems to be destroying every part of his life.

Then comes this ... . 'But this I call to mind, and therefore I have hope: the steadfast love of the Lord never ceases;

his mercies never come to an end; they are new every morning; great is your faithfulness. …'

Wow! The storm that besieges him has not slowed down, yet the flame of hope in the Lord's mercy, wisdom, power and sovereign control has not been extinguished. This man fights to believe even when struck down like this. The rest of the verses that follow verses 22–24 continue his faith-filled defiance of the seeming hopelessness of what he is experiencing. Read them when you can.

Yes, this was the prophet Jeremiah writing this. But yes, it is very like Christ on the cross, enduring God's punishment for His people's sins. And, O Lord, may it be us, when storms clouds rise and bring with them overwhelming difficulty. You are faithful to give us what we need, even if it only comes a thimble-ful at a time.

We praise You, creator behind the storm and calmer of every sea. Have Your way! Do Your will! Help us stand in defiance of doubts and fears. Make your resurrection power evident in our lowly, dead-ish lives today!

September 13, 2015
Big day today! First ultrasound and blood work since June and the great, sudden disappearance of the cancer. Will know in a week or so what they find. But whether it's back or not, I must say what a gift this summer has been! So many wonderful memories, many involving music and sweet friends. So nice having that rather than recovering from radiation treatment as was scheduled.

I am definitely fighting a bit of dread of what they may find with these tests … have to be honest there. But … If it is, then it is. And if it is, then I'm sure I will once more taste the deep sweetness of God's power and closeness that seem to come only with the bitterest cup.

It's not a small thing for me to say this, I know ... that He will meet me and carry me through whatever is ahead. There's more weight to that confidence than there used to be. Grateful that He's used this trial to grow my confidence in His ability and show me more of the extent of His dependability. Grateful that He's used this appointment today to show me that He really has grown me, even if just a little.

September 14, 2015

> Make a tree good and its fruit will be good, or make a tree bad and its fruit will be bad, for a tree is recognized by its fruit. MATTHEW 12:33
>
> I am the vine; you are the branches. If you remain in me and I in you, you will bear much fruit; apart from me you can do nothing. JOHN 15:5

Longing for both the fruit of my tree ... And the wood of it to be truly good to the core. Was reading about veneered wood furniture the other day. Apparently it uses only a sliver of beautiful, expensive wood glued to cheaper wood or even particleboard made from sawdust. Sometimes nowadays the veneer is not even made from wood but is some sort of man-made reproduction that simply looks like the real stuff. Wow! Fake on top of fake!

What a picture! Reminds me of the daily struggles in my heart. Oh, to not just know what it means to be God-centered, but to live, to think, to love God-centered...

from my center! Oh, to be truly, deeply good fruit with luxurious, rich wood from the bark of my words to the inner sap of my heart. I don't want to be veneer! I don't want to be particleboard! I don't want to be a tree of bad fruit! Oh Lord, graft your Son into me, even today. Let His roots and vine bear good fruit into my branches. Only through Him will it ever be!

September 21, 2015

God may take away the means of His provision, but never the promise of it. He will always supply what we need. And He is the one who loves not just with what He gives but in the when and the how in which He chooses to give it.

September 24, 2015

> For he spoke, and it came to be; he commanded, and it stood firm. PSALM 33:9

A great reason why we can go confidently through whatever lies ahead ... Not because we know what is coming ... Not because we can control it ... but because we are loved and cared for by the one who knows all and does all, wisely and perfectly ... And can do so by simply declaring it.

September 26, 2015

> The Lord lives. 2 SAMUEL 22

Feeding on this today. This one truth puts life and death and everything in between where it should be.

September 27, 2015

A BELIEVER by JOHN NEWTON

What a contradiction is a believer to himself! He is called a Believer emphatically, because he cordially assents to the word of God; but, alas! how often unworthy of the name!

If I was to describe him from the Scripture character, I should say, he is one whose heart is athirst for God, for His glory, His image, His presence; His affections are fixed upon an unseen Saviour; His treasures, and consequently His thoughts, are on high, beyond the bounds of sense.

Having experienced much forgiveness, he is full of bowels of mercy to all around; and having been often deceived by his own heart, he dares trust it no more, but lives by faith in the Son of God, for wisdom, righteousness, and sanctification, and derives from Him grace for grace; sensible that without Him he has not sufficiency even to think a good thought.

In short – he is dead to the world, to sin, to self; but alive to God, and lively in His service. Prayer is his breath, the word of God his food, and the ordinances more precious to him than the light of the sun. Such is a believer – in his judgment and prevailing desires.

But was I to describe him from experience, especially at some times, how different would the picture be?

Though he knows that communion with God is his highest privilege, he too seldom finds it so; on the contrary, if duty, conscience, and necessity did not compel, he would leave the throne of grace unvisited from day to day.

He takes up the Bible, conscious that it is the fountain of life and true comfort; yet perhaps, while he is making the reflection, he feels a secret distaste, which prompts him to lay it down, and give his preference to a newspaper.

He needs not to be told of the vanity and uncertainty of all beneath the sun; and yet is almost as much elated or cast down by a trifle, as those who have their portion in this world.

He believes that all things shall work together for his good, and that the most high God appoints, adjusts, and over-rules all his concerns; yet he feels the risings of fear, anxiety, and displeasure, as though the contrary was true.

He owns himself ignorant, and liable to be deceived by a thousand fallacies; yet is easily betrayed into positiveness and self-conceit.

He feels himself an unprofitable, unfaithful, unthankful servant, and therefore blushes to harbour a thought of desiring the esteem and commendations of men, yet he cannot suppress it.

Finally (for I must observe some bounds), on account of these and many other inconsistencies, he is struck dumb before the Lord, stripped of every hope and plea, but what is provided in the free grace of God, and yet his heart is continually leaning and returning to a covenant of works.

JOHN NEWTON, 'Cardiphonia' in *The Works of John Newton*, Volume 1 (London: Hamilton, Adams & Co., 1824), 1: 433-434.

September 27, 2015

COLOSSIANS 1:11 NLT

September 27, 2015

But he said, 'Oh, my Lord, please send someone else.'
(See EXOD. 3:7-12; 4:10-13)

Throughout this amazing encounter with the Lord, Moses does what we often do as we evaluate what God has put on our plates and how He has called us to respond. Moses omits the ultimate fact that changes everything about the way we think and should respond to God's call. That fact is not the difficulty of the calling or your perceived ability to answer that call. It is not the size of the situation or the size of your wisdom and strength. This life-changing fact is that the God of glory and grace, who calls His people to do His will on earth, always goes with them as they obey His calling. He never sends without going too. When He sends you, He doesn't give you a bunch of stuff to help you along the way. He always gives you Himself because He is what you need and He alone can give you what is required.

September 28, 2015

Once more, Mark's and my time away for a few days falls in the shadow of my cancer doctor appointment. Would you pray for these next few days for us to have a good time away and I leave Thursday's news for Thursday? Thank you! It's been a real struggle lately. Part physical, part spiritual. Learning that while the best trust looks like the rest of a weaned child on its mother's knee ... . that even the lagging, halting steps of a scared, weary, foolish, little sheep along the path behind the shepherd is a humble show of trust, too.

> But now thus says the LORD,
>> he who created you, O Jacob,
>> he who formed you, O Israel:
> 'Fear not, for I have redeemed you;
>> I have called you by name, you are mine.'

> ISAIAH 43:1

September 29, 205

> Trust in the Lord with all your heart and lean
> not on your own understanding. In all your ways
> acknowledge him and he will make straight your
> paths. PROVERBS 3:5-6

Trust in the Lord has three playgrounds inside of me: my will, my mind and my emotions. When all three are playing happily, I feel deep down peace and joy. But many times that third playground – my emotions will not play nicely. Like today, for instance. It is so discouraging how they lag behind in fear. But, I figure I can pray for those emotions, and will be grateful that both mind and will are standing upon the Lord's goodness. Perhaps the Lord will use them to join hands with my emotions and drag them in to play on the monkey bars at last. And if not, then so be it. Gonna keep fighting! Gonna keep living by what I know is true.

September 30, 2015

> May the God of hope fill you with all joy and peace as
> you trust in him, so that you may overflow with hope
> by the power of the Holy Spirit. ROMANS 15:13 NIV

Joy is knowing everything is going to be OK, even when everything isn't OK or might not be OK. And, it is a gift from the Holy Spirit. It has to be. In midst of struggling as I wait for the doctor's appointment tomorrow, God is kindly giving me tastes of joy today. I'm sure your prayers are part of this gift.

FYI ... . It may be a fine appointment. My ultrasound tech did do a lot of extra pic taking on the right side of my neck in three spots and that's what has me concerned. But it still may be all right.

> For to be sure, he was crucified in weakness, yet he
> lives by God's power. Likewise, we are weak in him,
> yet by God's power we will live with him in our
> dealing with you. 2 CORINTHIANS 13:4 NIV

October 1, 2015
Thank you, everyone, for praying for me! Just got back from the doctor with wonderful news.

Everything is still shrinking and my cancer marker numbers are great! I don't have to see her for six months instead of three. Next year will have the small dose of radioactive iodine and a scan again to check up-close on the little nodules. But just watch and wait for now. If that one goes well then it will be my last scan. Yay!

And she confirmed that a lot of my hyper anxiety is a side effect from the meds. (I tend towards anxiety about things, but this has been absolutely extreme!) She is willing to lower them a bit to see if I can get some relief from this daily struggle. it was wonderful to hear that there's a good chance that this will help.

Not too bad a present for my double nickels birthday smile emoticon Thanks again for praying and caring!

October 6, 2015

> Do not shrink, and suspect, and hang back from what it may involve, with selfish and unconfiding and ungenerous half – heartedness. Take the word of any who have willingly offered themselves unto the Lord, that the life of consecration is a deal better than they thought! Choose this day whom you will serve with real, thorough-going, whole-hearted service, and He will receive you; and you will find, as we have found, that He is such a good master that you're satisfied with His goodness, and that you will never want to go out free. Nay, rather take His own word for it; see what He says; 'If they obey and serve him, they shall spend their days and prosperity; and their years and pleasures.'

> FRANCES HAVERGAL, author of *Take My Life* and *Let It Be.*

October 17, 2015

What Daniel did when he heard of Nebuchadnezzar's demand to kill his wise men unless they tell him both dream and interpretation without him telling them anything: (from Dan. 2)

> 'Daniel went to his house and made the matter known to his companions and told them to seek mercy from the God of heaven regarding this mystery.'
>
> What the Lord did: 'Then the mystery was revealed to Daniel in a vision.'
>
> Daniel's response:

'Blessed be the name of God forever and ever, to whom belong wisdom and might. He changes times and seasons, he removes kings and sets up kings; he gives wisdom to the wise and knowledge to those who have understanding; he reveals deep and hidden things ...'

Seek mercy from the God of heaven about even the impossible! Pray! Don't be God's quality control and decide ahead of time what is too small or big for Him to do. He changes times and seasons. He sets up kings! He is able!

Blessed is the man who remains steadfast under trial, for when he has stood the test he will receive the crown of life, which God has promised to those who love him. JAMES 1:12

October 17, 2015

Psalm 106:

... they did not consider your wondrous works; they did not remember the abundance of your steadfast love. ... PSALM 106:7

But they soon forgot his works; they did not wait for his counsel ... . PSALM 106:13

They forgot God, their Savior, who had done great things in Egypt ... PSALM 106:21

They despised the pleasant land, having no faith in his promise ... PSALM 106:24

Remembering is crucial in trusting and obeying God. And at least for me, how much time I spend thanking God in my prayer times seems to have a direct correlation to how much I remember. Far more than sending God a thank-you note, He actually uses my thankfulness as fuel for my faith in Him. You want to trust God? You want more faith? Then spend more time thanking and remembering!

November 17, 2015

> C. S. Lewis called this anticipation Sehsucht, a German word for yearning. Sehsucht is used to describe a longing for a far-off country that's, for now at least, unreachable. Lewis connected the yearning itself and the foretastes of it with the joy that is longed for.
>
> *Happiness* by RANDY ALCORN

> O come, o come, Immanuel,
> And ransom captive Israel,
> That mourns in lonely exile here,
> Until the Son of God appear.
> Rejoice, rejoice, Immanuel,
> Shall come to thee, O Israel.
>
> 12th century hymn translated into English by JOHN MASON NEALE

> He will cover you with his pinions,
> and under his wings you will find refuge;
> his faithfulness is a shield and buckler.
>
> PSALM 91:4

DIARY
●●●●● **2016** ●●●●●

January 19, 2016

Thanks so much for praying! The Lord is helping me! One of the most helpful things has been thinking about the story of Jesus calling Peter to come walk out to Him on the waves of the Sea of Galilee. 'Look at me, not at the waves.' Helping me look to who it is who I depend upon, not on what is swirling around me and under me. In Him is all I need to face any storm. Focusing on His character, not my circumstance.

> The strength of patience hangs on our capacity
> to believe that God is up to something good for
> us in all our delays and detours.
>
> JOHN PIPER, www.goodreads.com

245

January 20, 2016

Dear friends, would you please pray for me? The Lord in His great kindness is bringing me through a season of great struggle with fear. I truly believe it is His kindness because I see where I hold onto things in ways that I should only hold onto Him. I want to learn to rest and trust in Him in these deeper ways and I'm pretty sure this is the only way to get there. But the struggle is so big and the path to get to where I want to go seems so unclear to me. But I know that when we pray, God hears and acts. Thank you so much!

January 30, 2016

Been struck by how much my trust in God looks like the little child scared of the water, yet learning to swim. He wants to swim. He has at least gotten in the water, but he is holding onto the side for dear life. Oh yes, over time he had gotten quite good at kicking his legs and sometimes paddling his arms, especially if his feet can feel the bottom of the pool or that little ledge at foot level in the pool. And yes, that is a bit of swimming.

But, oh, there is so much more! Requiring to push off into the water and leave behind side's security. And really learn to swim! Not left to figure things out on your own, but through your Coach. He will help, He will keep you safe. He will hold you up and giving you new abilities to stay afloat without any use of the old 'reliabilities' the side has to offer. And yes, sometimes you feel the water up your nose, but the delight of truly knowing what swimming is, is far better than what I've been doing holding on to the side. Trusting in God instead of what is typically depended upon for security is like this. I still do so much side-holding, but just lately have felt tastes of true swimming and it has been so wonderful. How good is the Lord! Oh, to know Him and trust Him more! Nothing like it. Simply nothing like it!

March 1, 2016

> 'Lord, he whom you love is ill.' 4. But when Jesus heard it he said, 'This illness does not lead to death. It is for the glory of God, so that the Son of God may be glorified through it.'
>
> Now Jesus loved Martha and her sister and Lazarus. So, when he heard that Lazarus was ill, he stayed two days longer in the place where he was.
>
> From JOHN 11

The One who loves us, most definitely answers us with 'wait.' And who but Him knows how to use 'wait' in such good and great ways! Today is a wonderful day to thank God for the 'waits' He has chosen for us … . While we are still in the midst of them.

March 11, 2016

> The Lord is represented as dwelling above looking down below; seeing all things, but peculiarly observing and caring for those who trust in Him. It is one of our choicest privileges to always be under the Father's eye, to never be out of sight of our best friend. …
> The eye of peculiar care is the glory and defense of God's people. None can take them unawares, for the celestial watcher foresees the designs of their enemies, and provides against them. They who fear God need

not fear anything else: let them fix their eyes of faith on Him, and His heart of love will always rest upon them. Our soul, our life, must hang upon God; we are not to trust Him with a few baubles, but with all we have and are. We, who trust, cannot but be of a glad heart, our inmost nature must triumph in our faithful God. The root of faith in due time bears the flower of rejoicing. Doubts breed sorrow, confidence creates joy.

C. H. Spurgeon

'Just a few baubles.' Wow! This cuts me to the heart! I keep trying to take back control of as much as possible and it is not needed, not wise, not best ... . and certainly not trusting.

Take my life and let it be,
Consecrated, Lord, to Thee ... .
Not a mite would I withhold ... .

Bold prayer, way outside of my spiritual 'pay grade' but praying that this would be my lip song, my life song AND my heart song.

March 30, 2016 – 7.54 a.m.
Trust in the Lord with all your heart and lean not on your own understanding. In all your ways acknowledge Him and He will make your paths straight. Proverbs 3:5,6

God's straight path is the way that takes us most directly through the good works He has prepared for us here and home to His arms. Sometimes it may feel like a tangly mess through heavy brush or impossibly hard to lift our feet through the mire of the path, but it is a good road and it is the best road and most of all it is HIS road!

And just to go on and mix in another analogy … . It's like standing with our faces one inch away from the Mona Lisa … . A lot of brush strokes, a little of color and almost no perspective. Step back! Step back! Step back with the eyes of faith. He is using it all for His grand, more-than-can-be-imagined purposes. And one day, the eyes of faith will be exchanged for true, full, complete vision. There will be no regrets. There will be nothing but amazement at all God was up to.

Feet to the path! Eyes to the skies! Hope in the heart!

March 30, 2016 – 8.56 a.m.
Psalm 118:4-8

4. Let those who fear the Lord say,
    'His steadfast love endures forever.'
5. Out of my distress I called on the Lord;
    the Lord answered me and set me free.
6. The Lord is on my side; I will not fear.
    What can man do to me?
7. The Lord is on my side as my helper;
    I shall look in triumph on those who hate me.
8. It is better to take refuge in the Lord
    than to trust in man.

Did you ever think about that 'What can man do to me' part even includes yourself? If you are someone like me who struggles just about daily now with what can be overwhelming bouts of anxiety (a side effect in my case of my personality and tendencies turbo-charged crazy high by my thyroid being gone and the effects of the high amount of thyroid meds they give me to keep cancer away), this is such a comfort!

God is even helping me triumph within myself in my inward struggles! He even sets limits on what the 'man' called me can do to me! The Lord is on my side on the inside! So even when the anxiety storms are blowing strong ... Which they likely will yet again today ... I can take refuge in the Lord and His ability to help me through and even use all of this to do good. So much to be grateful for!

March 31, 2016 – 10.31 a.m.

Praying that my eyes today would so be filled with glimpses of God and His goodness that it would be like deciding to take the pictures of the bride and groom before the wedding ceremony, instead of the first real glimpse of Him in His splendor be on that grand entrance day to heaven, whenever that is. His love and goodness show in His creation, in the love of friends, His Word, and in His Spirit inside ... as well as how He provides for us in so many remarkable, gracious and perfectly wise ways every day. They all show me what His heart is like.

So ... Looking for the trail of His rose petals down the aisle left for me to see as signs of His love. Still ... Face to face will be oh so wonderful, will it not!

> See, I am doing a new thing!
>> Now it springs up; do you not perceive it?
> I am making a way in the wilderness
>> and streams in the wasteland.
>
> ISAIAH 43:19 NIV

This little book has come to an end, but my journey with cancer and with God have not. The doctors continue to treat the cancer; I continue to need much grace as they treat. Will I ever make it to NED (No Evidence of Disease)? 'How long, O LORD?' is my cry, more days than I'd like to admit. And, while the LORD has yet to answer our prayers for a complete reprieve of these ailments, He most certainly has always given what is needed for each day's journey. He will hold me fast. He always has and He always will. And He will hold you fast, too, if you will but turn to Him and put your trust in Him.

Now to him who is able to do far more abundantly than all that we ask or think, according to the power at work within us, to him be glory in the church and in Christ Jesus throughout all generations, forever and ever. Amen. EPHESIANS 3:20-21, ESV

Acknowledgement

If I were allowed to thank only one person in the production of this little book, it would have to be Catherine MacKenzie. Catherine has been my fellow writer for children, my friend and sweet support for many years. She read my blog posts and prayed for me throughout the years of this journey. The idea for this book was her brain-child. She was not only the designer who saw the potential to join together the "fabric scraps" of my posts, but the seamstress who sewed them together into the coherent "quilt" you hold in your hands. Her artistry and added stitches here and there have made it more than I could have hoped for. Thank you, Catherine!

I'd also like to thank those who held my hand, dried my tears, cared for both my body and soul every step along the way of this journey. From my family, to all who read my blog and cheered me on, to the many friends and fellow church members here at CHBC, I have enjoyed such rich support. Blest be the tie that binds!

And thank you, Mark, my treasured husband. This has been your journey as much as mine. When you proposed marriage to me, you told me that you might not be the most spectacular catch, but would always be as faithful as an old shoe. If you are an old shoe, it would have to be one of Cinderella's glass slippers--one of a kind, and priceless. Shoe and prince among men, all in one. I love you.

And lastly, praise to the God and Father of my Lord Jesus Christ. You make my every boundary (even those of barbed wire) fall in pleasant places. And you promise me one day to get to live with you in a land that will be brighter than day, that will need no boundaries, and where there will be pleasures at your right hand forever. Oh, what a day! (Psalm 16:11)

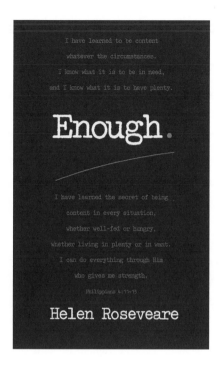

Enough
by Helen Roseveare

What is our motivation for serving Jesus? Is it so that we might have good health and be wealthy? Galatians 1 tells us that the wealth and health prosperity gospel is no gospel at all! However what we can find is fullness in Christ and in him we find that indeed God is enough for us! This easy to read book addresses key themes that span global cultures. It counters the view that material abundance is the sign of God's blessing and that poverty is a sign of God's curse. It teaches that contentment cannot be found in earthly possession, achievement or position, outside of God but can only be found in the fullness of Christ for every believer. We find in Christ that we have fullness and purpose.

ISBN: 978-1-84550-751-0

Christian Focus Publications

Our mission statement –

STAYING FAITHFUL
In dependence upon God we seek to impact the world through literature faithful to His infallible Word, the Bible. Our aim is to ensure that the Lord Jesus Christ is presented as the only hope to obtain forgiveness of sin, live a useful life and look forward to heaven with Him.

Our books are published in four imprints:

CHRISTIAN
FOCUS

Popular works including biographies, commentaries, basic doctrine and Christian living.

CHRISTIAN
HERITAGE

Books representing some of the best material from the rich heritage of the church.

MENTOR

Books written at a level suitable for Bible College and seminary students, pastors, and other serious readers. The imprint includes commentaries, doctrinal studies, examination of current issues and church history.

CF4•K

Children's books for quality Bible teaching and for all age groups: Sunday school curriculum, puzzle and activity books; personal and family devotional titles, biographies and inspirational stories – because you are never too young to know Jesus!

Christian Focus Publications Ltd,
Geanies House, Fearn, Ross-shire,
IV20 1TW, Scotland, United Kingdom.
www.christianfocus.com